You're Not Broke
You Have a Seed

You're Not Broke
You Have a Seed

Dr. Leroy Thompson Sr.

All scripture quotations are from the King James Version of the Holy Bible unless otherwise indicated.

ISBN 0-9632585-8-6

Ever Increasing Word Ministries

P.O. Box 7

Darrow, Louisiana 70725

Contents

CHAPTER ONE

The Spiritual Laws of Sowing and Reaping

One attribute of a seed is that it can multiply. The seed in God's system also has the ability to multiply. Now think about your money multiplying. When you understand the potential and power of the seed, you will discover how to sow yourself out of any financial dilemma. It's a fact that you cannot *work* your way out.

In the following pages I am going to share with you 1) the *purpose* of a seed, 2) the *process* of a seed, 3) the *power* of a seed, and finally, 4) the *sowing* and *planting* of a seed.

First, I want you to understand that there must be an exchange, and the seed is the method whereby you make this exchange.

Seedtime

While the earth remaineth, seedtime and harvest, and cold and heat, and summer and winter, and day and night shall not cease (Genesis 8:22).

The word "seedtime" is very important in biblical economics. There must be a seedtime, a time to sow your seed, if you are to have a harvest. And, to have a financial breakthrough, you must yield to the Spirit of God and allow Him to show you when it is time to plant a seed. A lot of people just want a harvest, but they must first have a seedtime.

In Matthew 25:21 we read, "Thou hast been faithful over a few things, I will make thee ruler over many things." God gives each one of us a seedtime, an opportunity to sow a seed. And He not only gives us the seed, but He will set us up with somebody to provide the right soil in which to plant this seed. You have to be looking for it, however. Most people are looking for harvest time, but seedtime precedes the harvest.

It is very important to study the timing of our sowing. We must plant the seed *when* God tells us to plant the seed—and plant it *where* God tells us to plant it. We shouldn't be concerned about what everybody else is doing.

This is an individual process. God can get us out of our financial straits while everybody stays stuck if we study the Word and do what God tells us to do.

Get This in Your Spirit—Seedtime

The Bible says in Acts 20:35, "It is more blessed to give than to receive." When we give, our giving will produce receiving. Giving also raises the level of receiving. Anyone can receive, but being a giver puts us in a position where things can be multiplied.

Let us look at the story of the rich young ruler, as told in Mark, chapter 10:

17 And when he was gone forth into the way, there came one running, and kneeled to him, and asked him, Good Master, what shall I do that I may inherit eternal life?

18 And Jesus said unto him, Why callest thou me good? There is none good but one, that is, God.

19 Thou knowest the commandments, Do not commit adultery, Do not kill, Do not steal, Do not bear false witness, Defraud not, Honor thy father and mother.

20 And he answered and said unto him, Master, all these have I observed from my youth.

21 Then Jesus beholding him loved him, and said unto him, One thing thou lackest: go thy way, sell whatsoever thou hast, and give to the poor, and thou shalt have treasure in heaven: and come, take up the cross, and follow me.

In this story, we see that we don't want to become wealthy on our own and from a secular standpoint because all that consists of is money. Even though we have plenty of money, if we don't understand seedtime, we will be miserable. We want the God-kind of money and we want it His way, so the blessing can stay upon us and our family and we can be happy. If we obtain wealth any other way, we will not yield it to God.

The rich young ruler could not adapt or submit to seedtime. We do not know how this young man obtained his wealth—whether he inherited it or came by it dishonestly, but we do know that he was religious. He went to church and he kept the commandments, but Jesus knew that he was weak in the area of finances. Many Christians today are also weak in this area. They are strong in other areas, but when it comes down to the area of finances they do not realize their weakness.

In verse 20, this young man said, "All these [commandments] have I observed from my youth." What we have here is an example of the present-day church. We keep all the commandments, but when it comes down to this money business, we think we can go another route. We say, "I'll serve you God. I'll sing, I'll pray and I'll praise," but when it comes down to money, we say, "I can handle this." Or we expect God to back us up through prayer, but prayer alone cannot change our finances. "I thought prayer changes everything," you say, but prayer alone will *not* change our finances, nor will singing nor taking communion nor going to church. Only *sowing* and *seed* changes our finances.

This young ruler religiously kept the commandments and we may do the same today, but we still can't go on our own. Wicked folks may go into business and make money right away, while a Christian has to pray all night trying to get a breakthrough. Why? Because money is no good without God governing that money. Therefore, God protects His children from money until we understand that we are not to be the servant of money; rather, money is to be *our* servant. God has governors on us protecting us and will not let us go the route of wealth *unless* we let the Holy Ghost *escort us into wealth*. This secret will cause us to move out into a realm of financial freedom with God. *We have to let the Holy Ghost escort us into the wealth of God.* The Holy Ghost will be our tutor and He will train us how not to let money take us over.

When you ask the question, "Why isn't my money coming to me? I have everything straight, why don't I have financial freedom?" you have to make sure that what you have now is *totally* turned over to God. Once you have turned *everything* over to Him and trust Him, He will escort you step by step, level by level, into His wealth.

We know He wants us to have wealth, according to 3 John 2,

> **"Beloved, I wish above all things that thou mayest prosper and be in health, even as thy soul prospereth";**

and Deuteronomy 8:18,

> **"But thou shalt remember the LORD thy God: for it is he that giveth thee power to get wealth, that he may establish his covenant which he sware unto thy fathers, as it is this day";**

and Ephesians 3:20,

> **"Now unto him that is able to do exceeding abundantly above all that we ask or think, according to the power that worketh in us."**

We see in these scriptures that wealth is not a problem with God, but many of God's children are still struggling in the area of living an average life. If you and I don't permit God to carry us into that secret place of His wealth, it will cause the visions of God and the works of God to suffer.

God does not want us to raise money for the church, He wants us to learn these wealth secrets—and one of these secrets is that the Holy Ghost will have to escort us through the seedtime period to get us ready for the wealth period. We must understand that everything we have comes from God. Many people in the Bible had money, like the rich man, Lazarus, the rich young ruler, and the rich farmer described in Luke 12:16-20:

> 16 And he spake a parable unto them, saying, The ground of a certain rich man brought forth plentifully:
> 17 And he thought within himself, saying, What shall I do, because I have no room where to bestow my fruits?
> 18 And he said, This will I do: I will pull down my barns, and build greater; and there will I bestow all my fruits and my goods.
> 19 And I will say to my soul, Soul, thou hast much goods laid up for many years; take thine ease, eat, drink, and be merry.

20 But God said unto him, Thou fool, this night thy soul shall be required of thee: then whose shall those things be, which thou hast provided?

In this story the rich farmer didn't say anything about how God had helped him, because he got his money the wrong way. You don't want to obtain your wealth the wrong way—you are better off broke; you want it by the Spirit. You must put God first in your finances, and your spirit has to be properly trained at the beginning so when that money starts coming in, you will not forget where it came from.

As God escorts you into His wealth, He will continue to be your companion, telling you what to do. Every level you get to, you will need more spiritual strength, more spiritual knowledge and more spiritual understanding. We can move from one level to the next, but it must come through seedtime, and we'll need the escort of the Holy Ghost to keep Satan out of our business.

Money without God means a *party* for Satan in our family. That is why we need to be governed under God before He can let us go. We have to fulfill the requirements He has set before us. If He lets us go before fulfilling the requirements, we do not have enough in us to maintain our walk with him. The further we get out into that financial arena, the bigger the demon that will come after us.

Let's go back to the rich young ruler. He couldn't handle his wealth, it was too much for his mind, so his riches overtook him. They were his master. We may be better off where we are than to receive wealth without the escort of the Holy Ghost.

Now say, *I'm not broke; I have a seed!*

We are talking about a supernatural seed. When it is placed in the hands of God, it produces supernatural results and it brings forth a supernatural financial lifestyle. You will not be normal anymore, you will not be average anymore. This supernatural seed will force out the average life.

In Mark 10, verse 20, the young ruler said to Jesus, "Master, all these [commandments] have I observed from my youth." The Holy Ghost is showing us that God, through Christ, is trying to bring this young man to seedtime in order to protect him from the money that he has. When you are dealing with big money, you have to be protected by God or you will begin to think you are God yourself. We see in verse 21, "Then Jesus beholding him loved him, and said unto him, One thing thou lackest," here is a man with money but also lack. This shows us that not everybody who has money is fulfilled. When you get wealth God's way and begin to walk in godly finances, you have God with you and you will not lack. Here is a rich man broke, but you're not broke because you have a seed! As we read on in verse 21, "Go thy way, sell *[seedtime]* whatsoever thou hast, and give to the poor, and thou shalt have treasure in heaven: and come, take up the cross, and follow me." Jesus told that man to plant a seed.

Why didn't the rich young ruler plant that seed? Because he didn't understand the seed principle. That is why many of us can't go some places we want to go because we have to learn the lesson. First, it is "not by might, nor by power but by my Spirit, saith the LORD of hosts" (Zechariah 4:6).

All the things God does in your life are by spiritual principles—not by might, not by power, but by His Spirit. In the same way, this financial thing is not by might, nor by power, but it is also by God's Spirit. So here *seedtime* has come to this rich man and he can't go there.

Now let's consider the church. Many times seedtime comes to the church and they can't go there. The first reason is because of fear. They are trying to hold on to what they already have. Second, they do not understand what God is trying to do for them, so they hold on to what they have to survive.

The Body of Christ is not supposed to be just *surviving* financially. We are supposed to be reigning *supernaturally* in our finances and God makes it possible.

SEEDTIME! SEEDTIME! SEEDTIME!

We must remember to study, listen to the Holy Ghost, and yield to Him at every turn when He tells us it is seedtime.

The Lord wanted this young man to see and understand what money was for in the earth realm to get his work done, but he couldn't yield to him because he obtained his money the wrong way as happens sometimes when people receive a lump sum of money. A woman in my church came into a large sum of money and she thought I wanted it. No! She needed to give, but she died worrying over that money, hoarding over the money she got.

To some people seedtime is a sad time when it should be a shouting time. You can sow your way out, but God is not going to let you work your way out by jobs. If you work your way out, you will not have the grace you need to maintain your walk with God.

You're Not Broke; You Have a Seed!

Let's look at verse 22: "And he was sad [*Who was sad? The rich young ruler*] at that saying [*What saying? Jesus told him to give—it was seedtime; this is three quarters of the church because they don't understand seedtime*], and went away grieved, for he had great possessions."

Why was he sad? 1) He didn't understand seedtime, and 2) He saw *giving as loss and not as gain*. For example, when it is time to give and you give $100, that $100 is not leaving you. Using the laws of God, it has just become your employee. It will begin to work for you as a servant to make money for you and bring it back to you.

Just as a businessman does, you need to keep up with your employees to know how many dollars you have out there working for you in the realm of the Spirit under the law of seedtime and harvest. As you sow a seed, write it down so you will know when you gave it. Carolyn and I began to keep a record of our giving and receiving, but God out gave me so much, I stopped keeping a record. His side far outweighed my side. Now I just do what He tells me to do by faith because I am totally convinced it works. But try this, keep up with your employees for a while. As you plant in this ministry or another ministry, follow the results you get from those employees. Money is your servant, you are not money's servant. The young ruler became money's servant instead of it being his servant. That is why he was grieved because he didn't understand seedtime.

As you read further about the young ruler, you will see that Jesus was saying, in essence, "Let Me take you over into My system so you can have the whole thing." Verse 22 says that "he went away grieved for he had great possessions," but really great possessions *had him*. "And Jesus looked round about, and saith unto his disciples, How hardly shall they that have riches enter into the kingdom of God!" (verse 23). Here He is referring to riches that are not governed by His Spirit, riches that did not come by God's way, riches that Satan can get his hands on and fool you that everything is all right.

When Solomon said in Ecclesiastes 10:19 "money answereth all things," he was talking about *natural* things. We don't need just natural things because money can't buy joy, money can't buy peace, and money can't buy love.

Let's keep reading. Verse 24 says, "And the disciples were astonished at his words. But Jesus answereth again and saith unto them, Children, how hard is it for them that trust in riches to enter into the kingdom of God."

How is God going to keep me from trusting in riches? *Through seedtime.* I know it is He who brought me into my wealthy place; therefore, my allegiance remains with Him, not with money. God has to have a pathway for you to know where you came from and that you love Him more than anything else. He does not want us trusting in money.

People think because I talk about money that I love money. No! I have an assignment from God to get the Body of Christ out of this hole. Many preachers don't understand me, but I'll get their vision fulfilled. I'll get money in their people's pocket so when the preachers come up with a vision, their people will have the money to write the checks, instead of the leaders having to beg for the Lord. God wants *us* ruling His work down here, not the president. There are so many misinformed preachers. They want the money, but they don't want *you* to have any. They want the Cadillacs but they want you to have a Chevy. But why can't we *all* have these things? We are not to hide God's blessing. How can they see Abraham's blessing if it is hidden?

Verse 26 says, "And they were astonished out of measure, saying among themselves, Who, then, can be saved?" Why would they ask this question? If they were not rich, they actually could not see anybody who was not rich. As far as that statement is concerned, all of God's children should be rich. What they were saying is, We don't know anybody broke. We are all rich. Are you telling us none of us are going to be saved? "And Jesus, looking upon them, saith, With men it is impossible, but not with God; for with God all things are possible" (verse 27).

You're not broke; you have a seed! And your seed is powerful! God is revealing to us divine principles He wanted to use to bring the rich young ruler into the hundredfold return. The ruler thought he had money, but God was trying to switch him from the world's system from which he got his money to His system where he really could have some money. But he couldn't pass the test. Don't let anyone tell you that there is no such thing as a hundredfold return. Whose words are you going to believe? Don't put so much confidence in men to where they have so much control over you that you can hear them louder than God.

Let's read on.

> 28 Then Peter began to say unto him, Lo, we have left all, and have followed thee.
> 29 And Jesus answered and said, Verily I say unto you, There is no man that hath left house, or brethren, or sisters, or father, or mother, or wife, or children, or lands, for my sake, and the gospel's (Mark 10:28-29).

Hear this very well. Do you remember when God called Abraham out from his kindred and from his father's house? He did this because He could not do what He wanted to do for Abraham there. The reason that many today are not walking in the hundredfold return is that they won't let God call them out.

God is calling us out, and the reason we have not had our breakthrough is that we are expecting somebody else to go with us. We still want to vote, we still want a second motion, but we have to go when God tells us to go. This is a personal thing, not group therapy. God is calling *you* out.

"Now the Lord had said unto Abram, Get thee out of thy country, and from thy kindred, and from thy father's house, unto a land that I will show thee" (Genesis 12:1). What is happening here? God is telling Abraham, "I can't show you until you get out. You cannot get to the hundredfold unless you get out. You have to come out from among those unbelievers and doubters and traditional people." He called Abraham out so he could do something extraordinary. That is why we cannot let other people govern our life; we have to come out ourselves.

Now let's go to Mark 10:29-30 where we have the Lord Jesus Christ saying basically the same thing that God said to Abraham:

29 Verily I say unto you, There is no man that hath left house, or brethren, or sisters, or father, or mother, or wife, or children, or lands, for my sake, and the gospel's,

30 But he shall receive an hundredfold *now in this time*, houses, and brethren, and sisters, and mothers, and children, and lands, with persecutions; and in the world to come eternal life.

In Genesis, God told Abraham, "I can't bring you to the hundredfold unless you get out of your house." So God brought him out and we see in Genesis 13:2 that Abraham was very rich because he came out when God called him out.

Mark 10:29 and Genesis 12:1 are saying the same thing: We can be rich here on the earth and go to heaven, too. Mark 10:31 says, "But many that are first shall be last; and the last first." This is referring to those who have been at the bottom from a spiritual perspective on the money end, especially the people in the church.

Why would God use these words "the first shall be last; and the last first" in this context with money? He is saying that many who didn't have money will have money, and the ones who had money will be under them. Jesus said "hundredfold." Whose words are you going to believe? When Jesus talks about thirtyfold, sixtyfold, and hundredfold in Matthew 13:8, these are not God's measurements as my God is *unlimited*. The hundredfold cannot measure God's ability to supply things in your life because He is the God of the overflow. The hundredfold is just to let us know where we are, and the thirtyfold, and sixtyfold are just to school us.

Another thing that we have made normal is the passage in Luke 6:38:

> **Give, and it shall be given unto you; good measure, pressed down, and shaken together, and running over, shall men give into your bosom. For with the same measure that ye mete withal it shall be measured to you again.**

We have made this verse traditional in that we have placed traditional values on it. But as we saw earlier, our God is unlimited; He is the God of the overflow. He tells us that we can have houses and lands and it doesn't bother Him—as long as we let Him stay in control of our life.

We are still dealing with seedtime here; we haven't gotten to harvest yet. The first word in this passage is "Give"—this is when God provides the soil for us; "Give"— as in, it is more blessed to give than to receive. Jesus said "Give"—seedtime! When seedtime comes in your life, God says "Give." And He says, "Don't you ever try to calculate My harvest because you can't. Every seed is a potential seed of the overflow.

Now let's look again at what God says in Luke 6:38: "Give, and it shall be given unto you; *[the only thing you did was give]* good measure, pressed down, and shaken together, and running over, shall men give unto your bosom. *[Here He is saying, "Men will have no choice because I will charge them to give to you."]* For with the same measure that ye [measure] it shall be measured to you again" (Luke 6:38).

Second Corinthians 9:6-7 says that "He who soweth sparingly shall reap also sparingly; and he who soweth bountifully shall reap also bountifully . . . God loveth a cheerful giver." The seedtime is God's way of dealing with this process. God is ministering to you so do not take it lightly. The Holy Spirit is producing some things in your life, and when He is finished, even your own family will not know you.

Look back at Genesis 12:1 and Mark 10:29, connect them together, and receive that revelation in your spirit. God calls us to give. He will provide soil for us when we get in a tight spot. He will sustain us, and give us more than enough.

Confess this:

Sweet Holy Spirit, show us what to do so we may walk in the financial fullness that You have placed upon us. Sweet Holy Spirit, You are our teacher. Show us divine secrets, rain on us with wisdom and understanding in this area where we will never be robbed another day in our life. We listen to You as You minister to us the principles and secrets that You are unfolding to us, and we declare that our lives will never be the same.

CHAPTER TWO

===

Seedtime Is Prime Time to Your Financial Future

The Spirit of God said to me that *seedtime is always prime time to my financial future.* And *prime time* is the most precious time to *your* financial future. Harvest time is not the most precious time, because the harvest came from the prime time, but *seedtime* determines or destroys your financial future. Either it determines how your financial future will come out in the supernatural, or it destroys your financial future if you do not obey the bidding of the Spirit to sow at a certain time—whether it looks good or whether it looks bad.

With that in mind we have discovered in Genesis 12:1 and Mark 10:29 that God called you out for a reason when He is ready to replenish or restore what is rightfully yours from the Garden of Eden. Adam was a rich man; he was surrounded in the garden by gold, but he lost it all when he sinned. Jesus came to restore everything that was lost in the Fall. We have record of this in 2 Corinthians 8:9:

"For ye know the grace of our Lord Jesus Christ, that, though he was rich, yet for your sakes he became poor, that ye through his poverty might be rich."

Most of us sow because of illiteracy, others because of ignorance in the Spirit realm about finances and our theological concept about God (the theologians really have messed us up). Most of us, however, sow out of famine. If we don't have anything, it's just like a famine. We have false prosperity—owning things that we buy on credit— but let us deal with reality because that is not prosperity. And remember, a revelation always has requirements.

Genesis 8:22 says, "While the earth remaineth, seedtime and harvest, and cold and heat, and summer and winter, and day and night shall not cease."

Note the last three words "shall not cease." Everything that falls into a category before those last three words still exist.

How do we sow in a time of famine?

When God tells us to sow, we shouldn't be using our condition as an excuse not to sow. Remember, *seedtime is always prime time to your financial future.* Whenever God gives you the opportunity to sow, no matter what condition you are in, sow that seed. It is the prime time to your breakthrough, prime time to your debt cancellation, and the prime time to convert you out of the system into the divine financial plan of God.

That seed has so much to do, because God comes to the point in your life that He can do something for you without argument and accusation from the enemy. Now you are giving Him the privilege to be God in that area of your life through supernatural manifestations.

Confess this:

Seedtime is always prime time to my financial future!

It is crucial that we hear what the Spirit of the Lord is saying. There may have been a time in our life when He told us to plant a seed in certain soil and we didn't obey. This disobedience caused us to be in financial trouble with God, and that is why we don't have the money we should be operating in. So when offering times come around, we say to ourselves, "I have sweated for this money," and we don't want to turn it loose. The Lord is revealing to us that this is like sowing in a time of famine.

The majority of believers are not living the life God wants them to live in this financial area because they have been cut off by tradition, by religion, by denomination, and by half teachings. You bring your tithes to the storehouse, but now it is time to see some results. The average Christian is actually sowing in the time of famine. If you experience the truth of this revelation, you won't go broke.

Seedtime is always prime time to your financial future! We see this in Genesis 26:1-5:

1   And there was a *famine* in the land, beside the first famine that was in the days of Abraham. And Isaac went unto Abimelech, king of the Philistines, unto Gerar.

2   And the LORD appeared unto him, and said, Go not down into Egypt; dwell in the land which I shall tell thee of:

3   Sojourn in this land, and I will be with thee, and will bless thee; for unto thee, and unto thy seed, I will give all these countries, and I will perform the oath which I sware unto Abraham thy father [this includes us] (*emphasis added*).

4   And I will make thy seed to multiply as the stars of heaven, and will give unto thy seed all these countries; and in thy seed shall all the nations of the earth be blessed;

5   Because that Abraham obeyed my voice, and kept my charge, my commandments, my statutes, and my laws.

Abraham obeyed God and that is why he was rich. We must understand God's primary requirements: obey His voice, keep His charge, keep His commandments, keep His statues, and keep His laws. That is the only way He can bring you out. You can't ignore what God tells you to do.

The Lord told Isaac, "I am going to do this for you, and you don't have to leave this land to prosper." Nor do we have to leave our physical location; the only thing we have to do is learn how to operate properly in the Spirit.

When the Lord told me He was going to do it in Darrow, He said, "You have to move in revelation, not in position, and the rest will take care of itself."

In that land of famine God promised Isaac abundance. Read verses 2 and 3 again:

2 And the Lord appeared unto him, and said, Go not down into Egypt; dwell in the land which *I shall tell* thee of:

3 Sojourn in this land and *I will* be with thee, and will bless thee; for unto thee, and unto thy seed, *I will give* all these countries, and *I will* perform the oath which I sware unto Abraham thy father.

Now let us go to Romans, chapter 4, which describes a climatic moment of a man fathering a child when he was not able, but God made it possible. Isaac was born by supernatural means. Let's look at verses 20 and 21:

20 He staggered not at the promise of God through unbelief; but was strong in faith, giving glory to God;
21 And being fully persuaded that, what he had promised, he was able also to perform.

Today, in the midst of your financial famine, He wants you to be fully persuaded that He is able to perform on your behalf what He has promised you. Prophetically, I speak to you that *seedtime is always prime time to your financial future.* I look at Christians all across the country who believe that God can do everything, but they are not fully persuaded of all the hundreds of promises He made in this area.

"You're not broke; you have a seed," and that seed will bring you out of any famine. It will get you off welfare and government cheese. It will bring you out of average financial living. You have dreams, you have desires, you have wants, and you have needs, but none of these are a problem to God.

Declare: *The Spirit of the Lord is upon me! My financial famine is over!*

A famine is when you may have a good job, but you're barely keeping up with your bills. Right here and now, let the Spirit of God breathe upon you and bring forth in your midst the power to walk out of any financial famine. The famine in your life can be over!

What do you do in a famine? How can you get out of a famine? Let's go to Genesis 26:12, "Then Isaac sowed in that land [that land where God told him to stay] and received in the same year an hundredfold." But that wasn't all he received—"and the LORD blessed him." I believe the Lord gave him another dimension of the anointing in prosperity because he obeyed in that hour. God gave him a *hundredfold* and *blessed him*. Could it be that the Lord said to Isaac, "The hundredfold will be a common thing to you because you have moved in greater territory."

Notice what happened in verses 13 and 14:

13 And the man [became] great, and went forward, and grew until he became very great:
14 For he had possession of flocks, and possession of herds, and great store of servants: and the Philistines envied him.

Seedtime is always prime time to your financial future!

What does *prime time* mean? It's the right time, opportunity time. We have switched systems and gone the world's way by the might of our own hand, trying to sustain our same lifestyle. "And thou say in thine heart, my power and the might of mine hand hath gotten me this wealth" (Deuteronomy 8:17). That wealth will not produce the type of wealth that you desire because you are born of God's Spirit. You have to live a supernatural lifestyle. But remember what the Lord has revealed to us—most of us are required to sow in the time of famine.

We see in Psalms 126:1-3:

1 When the LORD turned again the captivity of Zion [financial lack is a type of captivity], we were like them that dream. [The Lord is leading you today into your dreams.](*emphasis added*).

2 Then was our mouth filled with laughter, and our tongue with singing: then said they among the heathen, the Lord hath done great things for them. [The Lord has done great things for <u>put your name here.</u> When the heathens ask you who is doing all of this for you, you can tell them, "There is a man called Jesus who saved me from this rat race.] (*emphasis added*).

3 The LORD hath done great things for us; whereof we are glad.

It is time to shout. It has been revealed to you that *you are not broke; you have a seed.* Seedtime is a spiritual law that has been set up by God. If you follow it, nobody can stop it. *Seedtime is always prime time to your financial future.* You have found in Genesis 26 a man in the second famine and the Lord blessed him right in the famine. And the psalmist reveals to us that because "the LORD hath done great things for them," it made them glad.

Look at Psalms 35:27:

Let them shout for joy and be glad, who favor my righteous cause. Yea, let them say continually, Let the LORD be magnified, who hath pleasure in the prosperity of his servant.

Remember, faith shouts while the wall is still up. Shout! Shout! Shout! I am out of the famine! I have a revelation in my spirit and I am fully persuaded that what He has promised He is able to perform. I am out of debt! My house is paid for! I believe and receive it! I am going to shout in advance!

Let's read again Psalms 126, the whole chapter:

1 **When the LORD turned again the captivity of Zion [that is the church], we were like them that dream.**

2 Then was our mouth filled with laughter, and our tongue with singing; then said they among the heathen, The Lord hath done great things for them.

3 The Lord hath done great things for us; whereof we are glad.

4 Turn again our captivity, O Lord, as the streams in the south.

5 They that sow in tears shall reap in joy. [You who have sown out of a hard spot shall reap in joy. Those that sow even when it is hard to sow, because God told them to, shall return in joy with the harvest. Most of us are sowing from hurt, because we don't have enough to do what we need to do.] (*emphasis added*).

6 He that goeth forth and weepeth, bearing precious seed, shall doubtless come again with rejoicing, bringing his sheaves with him.

Your seeds are precious for two reasons: 1) You are sowing out of famine, and 2) You are obeying God. Your seeds are precious to you, to God, and to the soil in which you are sowing.

If you know how precious your seeds are to your financial future and sow that seed when God says to sow, you "shall doubtless" reap a harvest. Do not be "doubtless" about God's promises. We see in Romans 4:21 that Abraham was in the position of "doubtlessness" when he was 100 years old and his wife was 90, but God said, "Your wife will have a child."

Abraham trusted God, and so must we. We must say, "I trust God. I am not going to trust my body. I am not going to trust my banker. I am not going to trust my job. I am not going to trust somebody giving me a promotion. I am not trusting any man. I am trusting God! No more doubt about my financial issues! No more doubt about my financial condition! I trust God and, therefore, "I shall doubtless come again with rejoicing, bringing [my] sheaves with [me]." This is a sure thing.

If it is difficult for you to say, "I'm not broke, I have a seed," then 2 Corinthians 9:10 is the scripture that will help you: "Now he that ministereth seed to the sower both minister bread for your food, and multiply your seed sown, and increase the fruits of your righteousness." You must prove yourself to be a sower, or God is not obligated to give you seed.

Who is a sower? A sower is one who is operating under stewardship. What I have is not really mine. I am in management for Someone else, and whatever He tells me to do with whatever I have, I am willing to do it. God gives seed to the sower. If you become a sower for Him, your seeds will become bigger than the average person's harvest.

You are only going to sow in famine temporarily. You will soon come to the point where you will be searching for somewhere or somebody to sow in because your seed has gotten so big, the barn is running over and you are so busy planting, you don't have time to count the harvest. Also, the harvest doesn't mean that much to you anymore because you have become so wrapped up in being a sower and trying to fulfill the Abrahamic covenant, "Who can I bless?"

Let God get the weeds out of your finances that cause you to give sporadically and inconsistently. Let us become a bona fide sower.

CHAPTER THREE

Spiritual Laws Produce Supernatural Results

Spiritual laws produce supernatural results. This next spiritual law will give us insight into the world of God's provision that He has already provided for us as His children. Spiritual laws cause us to tap into another realm, another dimension, another lifestyle. They force us out of the life of average and push us into a life of the extraordinary, along with such people as the prophets of old, Abraham, Isaac, Jacob, Joseph, the little lad whose lunch Jesus multiplied, and Peter, who could catch no fish on his own but when Jesus sent him back, his ship ran over. We need to see more of that manifested in the lives of God's people today.

We have not seen this because of a lack of revelation, a lack of understanding, a lack of the anointing, and a lack of participation. But in obeying these spiritual laws, we can put ourselves in a position for the Holy Ghost to blanket us, to put us in a place for this type of financial anointing.

The struggle is over; restoration is here for the people of God. We have to walk therein by faith, and do whatever God tells us, believe in God, and trust in God. With no doubt, God said it; I believe it; that settles it.

Many times Smith Wigglesworth challenged people with two simple but powerful words—*Only Believe!* This alone is what God requires. Act upon whatever He tells you to do and He will manifest what He said.

In the first book of the Bible, God began to set up spiritual laws, one of which will never stop as long as the earth remains: "While the earth remaineth [Is the earth still here?], seedtime and harvest, and cold and heat, and summer and winter, and day and night shall not cease" (Genesis 8:22).

The Lord said that *seedtime* is always prime time to your financial future. In other words, the seed sets up the harvest. When you sow seed where God tells you to sow that seed activates supernatural provision from God as you obey Him.

In Isaiah 1:19, obedience is connected with seedtime. "If ye be willing and obedient, ye shall eat the good of the land." There are two requirements—"willing" and "obedient," then God says He will take over and you shall eat the good of the land. In the Living Bible, this verse reads, "If you will only let me help you, if you will only obey, then I'll will make you rich." The "rich" part is not the part that excites me, rather the part that says, "if you will only let me help you." The Lord is saying, "Let Me help you in this rat race."

Job 36:11 is a kindred verse to Isaiah 1:19: "If they obey and serve him, they shall spend their days in prosperity and their years in pleasures." The Living Bible translation says, "If they listen and obey him, then they will be blessed with prosperity throughout their lives."

I am a debt-free man, and I have removed myself from a life of average living. I am living an extraordinary life, and it is from the covenant found in 3 John 2: "Beloved, I wish above all things that thou mayest prosper and be in health, even as thy soul prospereth." Your mind, your emotions, and your will has to prosper, even as your soul has to prosper. Paul tell us to renew our minds with the Word of God. We need to renew our minds concerning God's provisions. Thousands of times He talks about what He wants to do for us. "The LORD is my shepherd; I shall not want" (Psalm 23:1) means He will provide for us.

Read Philippians 4:19 and the verses surrounding it: "My God shall supply all your need according to his riches in glory by Christ Jesus." We need to understand what "according to his riches in glory by Christ Jesus" means. We usually emphasize God's power and God's ability, but we don't take enough time to discover how much He really loves us and how much He wants us to have. His mercy and His grace is greater than His power. The Bible never says "God is power," but in 1 John, it says, "God is love." So because God loves me, I am going to delight myself in Him and He is going to give me the desires of my heart. Money is no problem with God, silver and gold is no problem with God, paying your bills is no problem with God, getting you out of debt is no problem to God. Only believe you can come out of debt with the Word of God. Increase your faith, increase your expectation, don't expect regular.

"According to his riches in glory." The question is, How much does God really have? Think about it: "According to his riches in glory." As believers we are not on the same economic scale of the world. The stock market does not run us. Our Father's provision is bigger than any company listed in the stock exchange. The biggest firm in Chicago or New York City pales in comparison to what your Father has, and it is your inheritance! Time is passing, so walk in the provision, walk in the anointing, walk in the awareness that God has provided so much for us that we will never be without. "I dare you to look at something and say I can't have it."

Another scripture that goes along with this is Ephesians 3:20: "Now unto him that is able to do exceeding abundantly above all that we *ask or think* [take note of these next words], *according to the power that worketh in us*". The revelation of this verse will never come to you if you don't know how much God loves you. If you read the scriptures preceding verse 20, God reveals how much He loves His children. Then, after revealing His breadth, length, depth, and height of love which passes all understanding, He says, "I am able."

I believe that power is twofold: *Our* part is walking in the revelation of His Word, the revelation of His provision, the revelation of His love, and the revelation of His anointing. And then *God* is able to do exceeding abundantly above all that we ask or all that we think.

There are many financial struggles, financial captivities, and financial strongholds in the Body of Christ which cause innumerable gifts to not be released because we are so busy working. There are financial burdens and yokes on people who really love God, people who have been tithing with no manifestation. Tithing, but the money isn't coming back. The windows of heaven do not open and so, eventually, people are going to cut back until they can find the real track. There are a lot of ministers that attack wealth. And if you attack wealth, you will attract lack. All of those people following them are going to have lack.

The Body of Christ has no business living
from paycheck to paycheck!

A problem is reflected in 2 Chronicles 20. There were five kings coming against Jehoshaphat. He consulted a prophet and the prophet told him what to do. The Bible says, "Jehoshaphat stood and said, Hear me, O Judah, and ye inhabitants of Jerusalem; Believe in the Lord your God, so shall ye be established; believe in his prophets, so shall ye prosper."

What has happened to many of us is that we are "established," but if we believe in His prophets, we shall "prosper." Let's see what happened in 2 Chronicles 20:25 when Jehoshaphat and his people believed the prophet and did what he told them to do.

> **"And when Jehoshaphat and his people came to take away the spoil of them, they found among them in abundance both riches with the dead bodies, and precious jewels, which they stripped off for themselves, more than they could carry away: and they were three days in gathering of the spoil, it was so much."**

This sounds like Luke 6:38, "good measure, pressed down, shaken together and running over"—God's overflow. God has no limits—"more than they could carry away."

Here we are talking about a whole army carrying stuff away. "They were three days in gathering of the spoil, it was so much." *All of this came from believing in God and believing in the prophet.*

It has been said, "He is the God of More Than Enough!"

There are some things we need to clarify that will make your life special. (And Christians are always special in God's sight.)

Never underestimate the power of a seed that God tells you to sow. "You are not broke" so stop going around telling everybody you are, and stop hanging around with those other folks who are broke. *You are not broke; you have a seed.*

I can prove that you are not broke. Every child of God has every seed God tells them to sow to activate His harvest power or harvest Anointing in their lives!

The Bible reveals to me that you have a "Harvest Anointing Seed" somewhere in your possession. You are not broke; but you keep listening to the devil. You have made some mistakes, bought some things on credit trying to prosper, and got yourself in trouble providing yourself with things. The Bible said you can have, but you did not obey the spiritual laws of God. Debt consolidation and debt cancellation are not the same thing. Consolidation is just juggling your debts from one side to the other side, but they are still there with added interest. What God is talking about is *supernatural debt cancellation* by the Holy Ghost acting on the Word of God.

Jesus told me that if I followed Him and pursued Him in this area, that I would be persecuted, but I don't care. I'd rather walk in my covenant and let God provide my needs than to please man.

When the hands of the Lord are upon you, you can outrun a chariot. If there was enough power in a dead prophet's bones to bring a man back to life, there ought to be enough power in a living prophet to bring you out of debt. I am telling you, you don't have to be broke anymore. Keep reading and only believe.

The Spirit of the Lord is upon you and a prophet wooing of the Holy Ghost is whistling over you. The Lord says, "They want to stand back and watch to see what happens, I'll show them." Men and women of God who know who they are and will start acting on the Word of God, will break all barriers and all road blocks and all boundaries, and they will flow freely into the things of God because I declare the hands of God's prosperity are upon you today!

All you have to do is believe and receive. The Spirit of the Lord is here right now to produce supernatural favor in your life, to produce supernatural increase in your life, and to produce supernatural debt cancellation in your life, so you can run and tell everybody, "Look what good things the Lord has done for me! Blessed be the name of the Lord!"

We are going to flee the doubt. We are going to flee the drought. We are going to take authority over the famine and we are going to call in plenty. And I declare, *MONEY COMETH to every person reading this now in the name of Jesus!* The Holy Spirit will not stop until you are financially free.

I know you have a seed, and there is such a thing as "eating your seed." If you don't eat that seed, but sow when God tells you, you can eat all you want. When I say "eating your seed," I am talking about *buying* something to appease the prosperity that is in you. However, you have to *sow* your way to the prosperity that belongs to you.

Prosperity will not be on you automatically; neither are you going to steal it. The spiritual laws must be obeyed, and we have to do what the Spirit of the Lord instructs us to do.

Now he that ministereth seed to the sower both minister bread for your food, and multiply your seed sown, and increase the fruits of your righteousness (2 Corinthians 9:10).

"Now he that ministereth seed to the sower [Are you a bountiful sower?] both minister bread for your food." So God will *feed you* and *keep you* while you are sowing and while you are eating from your divine supply of your divine provision. It is the Father's requirement between seedtime and harvest to take care of you.

Between your sowing the seed God gave you to sow (He promised after you sow the seed in obedience, He is going to feed you), take care of your business until the harvest. There should be no fear about this. If God tells you to do it, do it! Because He has somebody—perhaps a ram in the thicket—that He will use to supply you with food until your harvest comes.

Hear what the Spirit of the Lord is saying. "You can't get away from the seed. It is My way of doing things!" You cannot pray about this, you cannot look to your job or your education to produce a harvest. The Lord cannot break His laws that He has put into action for you. There are stacks and stacks of stuff with our names on them in heaven.

Verse 10 says, "and multiply." What does that mean? It means "increase" and it doesn't mean double. It is *more* than double. He said "multiply" meaning unlimited. "Multiply your seed sown, and increase the fruits of your righteousness."

CHAPTER FOUR

Understanding the Sower

He that observeth the wind shall not sow,
and he that regardeth the clouds shall not reap.
—ECCLESIASTES 11:4

The word "sow" means to plant seed for growth by scattering or to scatter (as seed) upon the earth for growth. The first thing you must remember is to always give God your best seed. To do that, you must listen to the Holy Spirit and do what He says. Sometimes the best seed may put a strain on you, but that is okay. Just do it. Give the Lord your "best seed."

Secondly, the sower's heart—that's yours—must be in your sowing. You must not sow as a ritual; for example, when offering time comes around, you just pluck a few bills in the bucket with the rest of the congregation because it is the right thing to do. No! The sower must know what he or she is doing. Sowers have *expectations* of harvest. Do you understand that? Every time you sow or everytime you plant, you make a demand on that seed and, therefore, you make a demand on the harvest. So don't turn it loose, and don't let the devil send you a seed and you call it a harvest. When it is a harvest, you will not be able to carry the same thing you carry the seed in.

Thirdly, understand the soil. As you are sowing to God the best seed, check out the soil. The seed and the soil never limit God. It is always Satan or the sower who limits God.

What does "he that observeth the wind" mean? It means if you are waiting for everything to get right before you start sowing—the economy, the stock market, your job, your boss giving you a raise—you will not sow. You must sow by faith, even though it looks like the factory you are working at is about to shut down. If God told you to sow that seed, sow it, because He is trying to get you out of that financial mess you are in.

Don't pay any attention to the clouds or the winds; just do what the Lord tells you to do. The wind of adversity is always blowing. Jesus said, "Whosoever heareth these sayings of mine and doeth them, I will liken him unto a wise man who built his house upon a rock" (Matthew 7:24).

You can put your finances in that rock. Jesus is the rock, and when you put your money in Jesus' work, it doesn't matter which way the economy is blowing because God is going to manifest himself in your life supernaturally.

"Supernaturally" means "above Satan." The devil himself cannot stop you once you are operating in the supernatural. It says in Romans 8:11:

"But if the Spirit of him that raised up Jesus from the dead dwell in you, he that raised up Christ from the dead shall also quicken your mortal bodies by his Spirit that dwelleth in you."

If that same Spirit has the ability and the power to raise Jesus from the dead, it also has the ability to raise my financial status.

You can't wait for a sunny day to sow. You must sow now, behind the revelation, and then expect God to do for you what He said. After all, didn't He feed three million people in the wilderness? He had wafers on the ground in the morning, and they were eating quail at dinner time. Nobody went hunting and nobody went to the store. God did it!

The Bible talks about that same three million in Psalm 105:37: "He brought them forth also with silver and gold: and there was not one feeble person among their tribes." Not one broke person among them. When they got to the Red Sea of adversity with Pharoah's army behind them, their God told the man of God—Moses—to stretch forth his rod, then He opened up the sea and made the bottom solid, and they walked on across. If that is the same God we serve today, I want to see Him in action. How about you? God is more than a shout and a fallout. He wants to fully deliver you if you let Him into every area of your life. I believe you ought to let Him!

Ecclesiastes 11:6 says: "In the morning sow thy seed, and in the evening withhold not thine hand: [withhold not thine seed] for thou knowest not [which] shall prosper, either this or that, or whether they both shall be alike good." What this means is to keep on sowing. Even when it looks like nothing is happening, keep on sowing.

I believe the bulk of the Body of Christ is in Genesis, chapter 26, because of theology, religion, tradition, and because of the doctrines of men and denominations. They won't teach you the fullness of the Word of God about your provisions because they have the erroneous concept that money is evil. Money is not evil; the Bible says the "*love of money* is the root of all evil". Money keeps your lights on. How can it be evil?

And how can money be evil when the Bible says money answers all things (Ecclesiastes 10:19). You ought to be able to see through that. What is evil is *not* to have money. Most Christians get in trouble at Christmas. They run everything through all the credit they can get and say, "I'll worry about it in January." So money is not evil and those days are over for you. *Money comes to you now in the name of Jesus! I'll never be broke another day in my life!*

Confess this:
I am a sower! Therefore, I will reap a harvest everyday!

I want to remind you that you can sow in famine when it looks like you have nothing to sow. Here is a revelation: Most Christians are in famine. They can't go anywhere; they have just enough to retire—if that. Young people work and they can't stop early enough to enjoy retirement. They have to work up until a certain age. There is no break and if they do stop, they have to get a part-time job to make ends meet.

This is so vital. You will have to sow yourself out of this famine that the church has put you in. I know you don't like it, but the church has gotten you into this dilemma by not telling you the whole truth. What does the Word say? "Now he that ministereth seed to the sower both minister bread for your food, and multiply your seed sown, and increase the fruits of your righteousness" (2 Corinthians 9:10).

There is so much the Lord wants to do for you. There is no shortage. Stop believing man and believe God.

Who Is a Bona Fide Sower?

Most of us are not bona fide sowers. We sow sporadically. Thus, God is not responsible to become our supplier. When you start sowing for a living, then God will become responsible for your giving. *A bona fide sower is one who sows consistently for a living.*

While you are sowing, God says He will "minister bread for your food, and multiply your seed sown." Then He will "increase the fruits of our righteousness." We see here the words "multiply" and "increase." Does that sound like God wants us broke?

Second Corinthians 9:11 says, "Being enriched in everything to all bountifulness, which causeth through us thanksgiving to God."

And Philippians 4:19 promises that "My God shall supply all your need according to his riches in glory by Christ Jesus."

God "shall supply all your need" if you become a sower, a bona fide sower. You cannot claim this verse if you are not a bona fide sower. This verse is speaking to a sower. If you study this text, you'll discover that these are people who have opened an account with God. When you open an account with God, it doesn't stay slack. God will fill your account.

"My God shall supply all your need" because you are locked in with His system. The sky is not the limit when you have huffed and puffed to make a decent living. You can't make a decent living on a check that your employers are giving you. What does God call a decent living? Go back and read about Abraham, Isaac, and Jacob. Isaac sowed in a famine and God gave him a hundredfold return.

So when you ask the question, How am I going to make it?, Say "I am sowing something." You must switch over.

CHAPTER FIVE

The Seed Process

Wherefore, if God so clothe the grass of the field,
which to day is, and tomorrow is cast into the oven,
shall he not much more clothe you, O ye of little faith?
Therefore, take no thought, saying, What shall we eat?
or, What shall we drink? or, Wherewithal shall we be
clothed? (For after all these things do the Gentiles
seek.) For your heavenly Father knoweth that ye have
need of all these things.
MATTHEW 6:30-32

In the above verses, God gives us the way to break out of our walls of containment and the way to get all of our needs met. The key, however, is in verse 33:

Seek ye first the kingdom of God, and his righteousness; and all these things shall be added unto you.

Notice the words "kingdom of God." What God is doing here is setting up a specific system to get those specific things that you need manifested. The process is called the "kingdom of God." Actually, what He is saying to His

children is "seek ye first My way of doing things."; The
job is not God's way. The job is not to make a living, it is to
get seed so you can *sow* for a living. Some say, "If I can
only get a good job. The job I have now is not a good job.
The pay isn't enough."

What is this process leading up to? Manifestation!
When you deal with God's system, you always go into the
"over and above." If you are not in the over and above,
you are in the wrong system. Many think because you have
$15,000 in the bank, that's it, but if God had a project, it
would be hard to give because it was a struggle to get it.
The job has limitations. How many of you are ready to
break through limitations?

What should you do when you have a need? There are
three rules to follow:

1. *Cast a seed into the ground*

You have to follow God's instructions. In Matthew 6:33
we see the kingdom of God, which is God's way of doing
things. We may have followed God's way in a lot of things,
but we have never tapped fully into His way of doing things
about money. What He wants us to do is to get what He
wants us to have.

Matthew 6:33 and Mark 4:26—"So is the kingdom of God, as if a man should cast seed into the ground"—both refer to the "kingdom of God." Luke also explains the process of what you have to do to switch from one system to another system. Now remember, "Seek ye first the kingdom of God and "so is the kingdom of God, as if a man should cast seed into the ground." What does a man do when he has a need? Work overtime; look for a second job.

The first thing in the process is to cast a seed into the ground. Note, however, that the worlds system will not tell you to do this. The worlds system tells you that you need a savings account and a budget. When you get on God's system properly, you don't need a budget. A budget is merely to stop you from overspending, but when you get into the system you can't overspend.   Now until you get out of the system, you will have to budget yourself. The key is to change your thinking because God is unlimited. You must do what He tells you to do to break out of these walls of containment.

You can plant a financial seed but if you let words come out the wrong way, you will uproot the seed with the words of your mouth.

Your words have been stout against me, saith the LORD. Yet ye say, What have we spoken so much against thee? (Malachi 3:13).

Let God become your source, plant your seeds, and pray in the Spirit. When a man is praying in the Spirit, the Bible says he is speaking unto God, not unto men. Hidden wisdom and hidden secrets are revealed. When you plant a seed, God will give you secrets about money, then you put yourself in a position to get the wisdom to know what to do while you are waiting for the seed in the ground to grow. The second thing praying in the spirit does is after you have planted your seed, it edifies, builds you up, and gets you ready to go through whatever you have to go through as a result of planting that seed.

You need wisdom in order to become wealthy, and wisdom is the ability to use the knowledge you need about money. Wisdom will show you what to do and how to do it. Also wisdom shines the light and takes all the knowledge you have obtained; plus, it will even give you knowledge you did not have in the form of revelation. All of a sudden, not only will you be able to do something you didn't know how to do. Then you will have a right to the harvest of what you now know how to do because you planted a seed.

This is very important. We saw in Matthew 6:33 where the Lord says, "Seek ye first the kingdom of God," and in Mark 4:26, we saw how the system works by casting a seed in the ground.

2. *Expectation*

When a man plants a seed, the first thing he does is to put himself in a situation to expect. Many times someone else is getting your harvest because you lost the expectation and God doesn't want the seed to go to waste. So somebody else is confessing and ends up taking your harvest. *Expectation! Expectation!* When do you expect to be out of debt?

Most people are not getting a harvest because they don't expect one. That boy at that gate in Acts, chapter 3, received his healing because he was expecting to receive something. You have to have expectation. If you don't plant, don't expect, but if you plant, expect.

3. *Name your seed so that you can recognize when it comes up*

The third thing to do is to name your seed so that you can recognize it when it comes up. If you are believing for $5,000 and somebody gives you $500, put the seed back in the ground. That is why men throw little fish back into the stream. The harvest is the word you spoke; give God time to do it. While you are doing that, He will feed you and take care of you.

If you are in debt but you have not planted a seed to get you out of debt, then you are not looking to get out of debt. The worlds system is set for you to stay in debt. Where there is no expectation, there is no need for fulfillment. What are you dreaming about? God said you can't dream any bigger than He can deliver. Don't settle for less because He has provided for you to have the best. The best is God's system, seedtime and harvest. We are not to tip God and pay the world; it should be the other way around.

Expectation that cannot be killed is expectation that cannot be denied. You have to have expectation. You plant the seed and expect God to come through as He has said, and He will come through every time. You must pass some tests, however. He will check you out over here and over there.

Once you have planted the seed, go to sleep. "Thou will keep him in perfect peace, whose mind is stayed on thee" (Isaiah 26:3). "Trust in the LORD with all thine heart, and lean not unto thine own understanding" (Proverbs 3:5). Build up your expectation and go to sleep. In other words, you plant your seed, then go about your Father's business, praising the Lord. "Oh," you say, "I have great expectations. My $45,000 is coming in, glory to God! I am going to pay off all my bills. Glory to God! I am going to dance out of the store when I pay them off." You have to have expectation.

"And should sleep, and rise night and day, and the seed should spring and grow up." If you do your job, the seed will do its job. Thank you, Jesus, we don't have to worry about what is going on under the ground with this seed, I can sow in one place and reap from another. Thank you, Jesus. "He knoweth not how." I don't know how my church got here, I don't know how it got full, I don't know how my closet got full. I just planted seeds, went to bed, went to sleep, got up, and praised the Lord. I shouted in my old house, woke up one morning, and I moved. Once you get in this system, you will be baffled by how God does things. *You're not broke; you have a seed!*

CHAPTER SIX

Don't Eat the Seed!

Now, concerning not eating the seed, what are we I going to eat? Eat the bread! Now if you don't understand what the bread is, the Holy Spirit says, "Eat the harvest, but don't eat the seed." A good farmer holds his best corn for seed and eats the rest. So you take the best out of your harvest for your seed, eat the harvest, and leave the seed alone.

Second Corinthians 9:10 says, "Now he that ministereth seed to the sower both minister bread for your food." Don't get the bread mixed up with the food. God will feed you and seed you, but you must know the difference between the feed and the seed. And most people eat it all up. "Now he that ministereth seed to the sower both minister bread for your food," and He is not through with you. "And multiply your seed sown"—He multiplies your seed sown, He provides you with bread, and supplies you with seed. He supplies and multiplies.

He can't multiply an "eaten" seed; He multiplies seed sown, not seeds eaten. The seed eaten goes out in the drought. God not only provides the seed, He provides the soil. We have to be sensitive to the Spirit, listening to whom or where He is telling us to sow.

God is not moved by a need, He is moved by a seed.

Let us look at this thing further. Not only does God provide the seed and the bread, and multiply the seed, He also supplies the soil. He supplies the place where you can sow and reap great dividends. He says, "He that ministereth seed to the sower both minister bread for your food, and multiply your seed sown, [where He tells you to sow it] and increase the fruits of your righteousness" (2 Corinthians 9:10).

He tells you what the results will be. You will be "enriched in every thing to all bountifulness, which causeth through us thanksgiving to God" (verse 11).

Then you will be ready to give towards everything the Lord wants to do, and laugh while doing it. It says in 2 Cor 9:8 "And God is able to make all grace abound toward you; that ye, always having all sufficiency in all things, may abound to every good work."

"Abound" means to increase greatly. You will be able to increase greatly in your giving. Things that God has going on, you will be able to jump right on them. "Another opportunity for me to plant more seeds," you will say. In this seedtime system, we can act and think like God.

In Isaiah 55:7-9, we see more about the seed:

7 Let the wicked forsake his way, and the unrighteous man his thoughts: and let him return unto the LORD, and he will have mercy upon him; and to our God, for he will abundantly pardon.
8 For my thoughts are not your thoughts, neither are your ways my ways, saith the LORD.
9 For as the heavens are higher than the earth, so are my ways higher than your ways, and my thoughts than your thoughts.

How often we have taken these verses out of context. The Lord here is talking about wicked folks, not His children. He is saying that wicked folks don't understand, they are confounded, can't get revelation and are confused. All we have to do is cooperate, and the Lord will tell us enough that we won't need to know anymore. He is in the business of revealing Himself to His children.

Verse 8 is talking about the wicked. They cannot have the thoughts of God, neither are their ways His ways. But we have God's thoughts because He has revealed them to us. His ways are our ways and our ways are His ways.

Uninformed carnal Christians fit here too. They are ignorant of the Word and ignorant of the truth, so they live like sinners. But as we have read, God is talking about His thoughts—how high they are, and His ways—how high they are. This is exactly what we are studying here. We are studying God's ways about finances, and they are a whole lot higher than your job. That is why you have to get in your spirit to be a bona fide sower or you will fall off of this. If you are going to really follow God's plan that will cause you to supersede the system, you will have to follow the command Mary gave the men at the wedding, "Whatever he saith unto you, do it" (John 2:5). Also Paul's request, "Lord, what wilt thou have me to do?" (Acts 9:6), and we will get the results the disciples received in Luke 5:6,

"And when they had this done, they enclosed a great multitude of fishes; and their net brake."

The ship did not run over and the net did not break until they obeyed.

Let's look now in Isaiah 55:10-11:

10 For as the rain cometh down, and the snow from heaven, and returneth not thither, but watereth the earth, and maketh it bring forth and bud, that it may give seed to the sower, [you sow the seed and eat the bread] and bread to the eater (*emphasis added*).

11 So shall my word be that goeth forth out of my mouth: it shall not return unto me void, but it shall accomplish that which I please, and it shall prosper in the thing whereto I sent it.

Don't forget we are talking about "don't eat the seed." Now let us go to Ecclesiastes 11:6:

In the morning sow thy seed, and in the evening withhold not thine hand: for thou knowest now [which] shall prosper, either this or that, or whether they both shall be alike good.

And Psalm 37:18-19:

18 The LORD knoweth the days of the upright: and their inheritance shall be forever.

19 They shall not be ashamed in the evil time: and in the days of famine they shall be satisfied.

In other words, if you get in on this system of seedtime and harvest—which is God's way of doing things—no matter who invades who, no matter what famine comes, what shortages come, you will see why you have to come off the system. The worlds system works only when the system is working right, but God's system works all the time because it cannot go wrong. We are not on the world's system. My check is not my source. You have to come to that conclusion, if not, when famine comes, you will be just like other people. If you wait until famine comes and then try to switch to God's system, it won't work because it will be more fear than faith. But, if you get it straight now and have already switched before the famine comes, you are already prepared.

This is one more reason to switch—because you want to obey God. Another reason is because the world's system can't supply enough for you to live like God wants you to live. And thirdly, if anything happens out of the ordinary, you don't have to be bothered about it. Why? Because God is your source. You made Him your source in a time when things were good.

So, as you are reading this, God is aiming to make you switch masters.

CHAPTER SEVEN

Never Underestimate the Power of a Seed

The seed is the essential element

of transmitting life

According to the Jewish way of thinking, they believe that because they were the chosen people, they were supposed to prosper in every area of their lives. That is why we have such a gap between the Old and the New Testament. The Old Testament Jews, the children of Israel, knew that God had provided a lot of things for them and they live in that lifestyle. Somewhere under the dispensation of this "Grace Period," the New Testament Church—which was supposed to have a "better covenant"—lost that vision. This has crippled the church and now it has to depend on the world's system for many things. And this is not God's will.

Some of you have been planting seeds and have not received a harvest. The "seed principle" is the most powerful principle in the Bible. This is because Jesus was called a "seed." *The seed is the essential element of transmitting life.* The "Word" is also called a seed. You need to recognize the fact that there is life in the seed principle and, unless you can see and understand this, you won't be able to receive the benefits from it. You will think it is just a good little scripture and try to do it. But you don't have to try to do it; it belongs to you.

Let's look at Galations 3:16:

Now to Abraham and his seed were the promises made. He saith not, And to seeds, as of many; but as of one, And to thy seed, which is Christ.

Notice that the first singular "seed" is talking about Christ. Are you with me? "As of many, but as one, and to the seed, which is Christ." Now look at Galations 3:19:

Wherefore, then, serveth the law? It was added because of transgressions, till the seed should come to whom the promise was made; and it was ordained by angels in the hand of a mediator.

God sent His life in the earth realm through a seed, and that seed was Christ. You are also called a seed. The "Word" is called a seed. The Holy Ghost wants you to ride piggyback on this revelation, to understand that it is not just talking about financial seed, but the Seed by which

God transmitted His divine substance and eternal life to us through His Son and the Word of God. Many times as we talk about raw finances, it turns people off, but everything starts off as a seed. Eventually, folks will appreciate God's way of doing things, come in agreement with His way, and reap the blessing therewith.

> **Being born again, not of corruptible seed, but of incorruptible, by the word of God, which liveth and abideth for ever (1 Peter 1:23).**

The "incorruptible seed" is the Word. In Mark 4 and Matthew 13, we see the parables that Jesus taught about the sower sowing the Word, here referring to the Word as the seed. You must understand the importance of a seed. John 12:24 tells us,

> **Verily, verily, I say unto you, Except a [grain] of wheat fall into the ground and die, it abideth alone: but if it die, it bringeth forth much fruit.**

This is talking about Christ's death—the way He died as a seed and how life came through His death. He was the essential element of transmitting life. This is supernatural—supernatural because God implemented it. If you don't understand this, you will underestimate it. This cannot be undone because the Lord said it. People can argue about it, come up with theological concepts, and do what they want to do, but the Lord says His way of transmitting life is through the seed. Also He says that you can plant financial seeds and transmit this type of harvest.

Farmers understand the seed principle. My daddy was a farmer and he planted every year. He started out by getting the barns ready, the sacks ready, the truck ready to haul to the place where he was going to sell it—everything. This is the way the church should be. It isn't hard. When the church starts thinking like the farmer, things will began to happen out of the ordinary.

Say this: *"Never underestimate the power of a seed."*

We were saved through the seed principle. Jesus became a human being through the seed of a woman. We have been giving and giving and giving, but we don't receive. We have to break this cycle. The only way we are going to do this is with understanding and the anointing and knowing how to put pressure on the Word. That is all the Holy Spirit is asking us to do. We are people of God, and God has set up things that we may be able to take care of His business, as well as our own.

There *is* power in a seed. This is shown in the following passage found in Ecclesiastes 11:1-3:

1 Cast thy bread upon the waters; for thou shalt find it after many days.
2 Give a portion to seven, and also to eight; for thou knowest not what evil shall be upon the earth.
3 If the clouds be full of rain, they empty themselves upon the earth: and if the tree fall toward the south, or toward the north, in the place where the tree falleth, there it shall be.

When you receive a revelation, you continue doing what you know to do, even though you don't see results, because you have done it by faith. This is not a swap exchange. It's God developing you to trust Him in any given area, and He wants you to trust your seed. He also wants you to know the difference between *seeds* and *weeds*. There are weeds that grow up and choke your seed, but you cannot be afraid and stop planting because of circumstances. A little pressure is good when you are growing into something. That way when you come out, you will know how it works. I want you to receive. Once you start receiving like you should receive, no one will be able to tell you anything.

He that observeth the wind shall not sow; and he that regardeth the clouds shall not reap (Ecclesiastes 11:4).

In the above verse, underline the word *wind*. There are many winds of adversity. Every time you think you are getting caught up financially, things start breaking down, somebody messes up, somebody gets sick, the kids need clothes. All sorts of things happen. You know what I'm talking about. It happens to all of us.

But remember, there wouldn't be a need if we didn't have an enemy. For every aspect of the covenant, Satan has a counteraction. When you start believing that you are going to live by this system, eight hours a day, forty hours a week, you are not going to be able to do what God wants you to do, because He wants you to be able to pinpoint His visions that He gave to you and send them out without any sweat. So don't be afraid of the system of seedtime and harvest or the seed principle when the wind is blowing.

"He that observeth the wind shall not sow, he that regardeth the clouds shall not reap." In other words, "I'll wait for good weather," or, "When I get all of my bills paid," or, "When the kids leave I'll do better." But you don't have to wait until all these things happen. Just obey God and have faith in what He tells you to do. Don't wait for good weather, don't wait for the wind to stop blowing. The wind is going to continue to blow, it's going to blow you right from your inheritance.

How many of you have ever observed the wind in finances? How many of you have seen the clouds? Boy, I have seen some clouds.

Remember, he who regards the clouds shall not have a harvest. If you don't sow, you will not reap. Nothing plus nothing equals nothing!

Let me give you a warning here. Never say you want your seed back. I once heard a minister say, "If I just had the seed back I have sown." I said, "Lord, what is he saying?" The man said, "If I had the seed back I've sown, I'd be satisfied." You don't want to say that. Even if you get that seed back, it is not going to be enough for what you are believing God for. I don't want any seeds back that I have sown. I want a harvest. What about you? If you have sown your financial seed and it becomes cloudy, don't watch the clouds and the winds. Watch for what God promised you.

Romans 4:21 tells us that we have to become "fully persuaded that, what he had promised, he is able also to perform." Put this verse in your spirit. You must believe that this promise also concerns finances. Finances are part of the covenant. What an awesome price Christ paid for us on the cross. He "has redeemed us from the curse of the law." Living in lack, insufficiency, barely getting by has no iota of royalty on it. You are not a king and a priest if you don't know how your covenant works.

Let's look also at Romans 4:17:

(As it is written, I have made thee a father of many nations) before him whom he believed, even God, who quickeneth the dead, and calleth those things which are not, as though they were.

Based on this verse, you have to believe and be fully persuaded before you call things that "be not as though they were." You have to call long enough before you believe what you're calling and then it will come.

Let us read a little more in Ecclesiastes 11. Verse 5 says,

As thou knowest not what is the way of the [wind], nor how the bones grow in the womb of her that is with child, even so thou knowest not the works of God, who maketh all.

Do you know how a baby grows in a woman's womb? This, too, is a seed and the Lord takes care of it. Ecclesiastes 11:5 is a powerful verse by itself, but if we read it along with Mark 4:26-29, we can see what verse 5 is really saying.

26 And he said, So is the kingdom of God, as if a man should cast seed into the ground;

27 And should sleep, and rise night and day, and the seed should spring and grow up, he knoweth not how.

28 For the earth bringeth forth fruit of itself; first the blade, then the ear, after that the full corn in the ear.

29 But when the fruit is brought forth, immediately he putteth in the sickle, because the harvest is come.

First the blade, then the corn, and the full corn in the ear. It was harvest time. He "putteth in the sickle," but he still didn't know how the seed grew.

So Ecclesiastes 11:5 and Mark 4:27 are basically saying the same thing. Don't pay attention to the wind and clouds, or let the devil tell you that you are a "money grabber" or a "money mongrel," or that all you think about is money.

Some of you have seed in the ground and those seeds are trying to spring up. Even though the seed may be in the ground under concrete, it will crack that concrete. My daddy told me that a long time ago and I never could understand it. I said, "What? Crack that concrete?", and he said, "Yes." The lesson here is that the concrete of the devil can't block your seed. It might take a little longer to come up, but it will come up. Right now, some of you have seed in the ground and that seed is working on that concrete. The devil may have put some extra layers of concrete on it, because he wants you to hold off. He knows if your seed comes up quickly, you will become contagious and start testifying and telling other folks what happened to you.

Why do so many people keep putting money in slot machines? Why do men and women take every check that comes into the house and go to the casino every week? Because they believe that they will hit the jackpot. They are trusting the devil more than God's promises. Just keep on sowing and keep on believing. You may have sown nineteen times, but don't give up. That twentieth time declares to God that you believe Him. And that may be the time God will work suddenly on your behalf.

This is what Ecclesiastes 11:5-6 is saying. Read it again:

5 **As thou knowest not what is the way of the spirit, nor how the bones grow in the womb of her that is with child: even so thou knowest not the works of God who maketh all.**
6 **In the morning sow thy seed, and in the evening withhold not thine hand: for thou knowest not [which] shall prosper, either this or that, or whether they both shall be alike good.**

It would not be faith if everything worked like flipping a dime. God has to allow you to see some wind and some clouds, but He will not let any of that stuff shake you. You will just keep on sowing because you have God's Word on it, "Whatever a man soweth, that will he also reap."

Don't ever underestimate the power of a seed. Always give God your best. Let's look at Mark 4:15-20:

> 15 And these are they by the wayside, where the word is sown; but when they have heard, Satan cometh immediately, and taketh away the word that was sown in their hearts.
>
> 16 And these are they likewise which are sown on stony ground; who, when they have heard the word, immediately receive it with gladness;
>
> 17 And have no root in themselves, and so endure but for a time: afterward, when affliction or persecution ariseth for the word's sake, immediately they are offended.
>
> 18 And these are they which are sown among thorns; such as hear the word,
>
> 19 And the cares of this world, and the deceitfulness of riches, and the lusts of other things entering in, choke the word, and it becometh unfruitful.
>
> 20 And these are they which are sown on good ground; such as hear the word, and receive *it*, and bring forth fruit, some thirtyfold, some sixty, and some an hundred.

Notice the word "soweth" in verse 14. "The sower soweth the word." Sowing finances is the same principle; it's just a different category of the covenant.

Now look at verse 15. "And these are they by the wayside, where the word is sown; [or where the seed is sown] but when they have heard, Satan cometh immediately and taketh away the word that was sown in their heart." In their heart! It took me years to get this.

Now go to Matthew 13:19.

When any one heareth the word of the kingdom, and understandeth it not, then cometh the wicked one, and catcheth away that which was sown in his heart. This is he which received seed by the wayside.

In his Gospel, Matthew deals with money as he was a tax collector. The Holy Ghost used him in this area. He says you can get robbed of your finances if you don't have understanding.

In Matthew 13:19, where it says, "When any one heareth the word of the kingdom," the "word" is the seed that was upon their heart but they did not understand. Satan takes away from you what you don't understand. Deception and ignorance are the two things he feasts upon.

He wants to deceive you, but if you have knowledge of God's Word, he can't deceive you and he can't take it away from you.

Let me tell you this, you will have to take your finances by force. What kind of force? Revelation knowledge and the anointing. You are going to have to use these two forces, along with the energy of the Holy Ghost, to take what is rightfully yours out of your covenant. Just tell Satan, "I have a covenant with Almighty God!"

Everything that works against the Word as a seed works against your financial seed. So the first power the devil uses against the church in the area of finances is the lack of understanding. Go back to when you used to think a certain way about your finances, how you were taught. We didn't know about our covenant; we were ignorant of it. The only thing we need to do is to apply our faith, and not try ourselves to make it happen. Let God make it happen. Just do what He tells you to do and He will take care of the rest.

Another attack of the enemy is found in John 10:10: "The thief cometh not but to steal, and to kill, and to destroy." Satan will attack you, especially when you see the light and are about to move out in that light. He will attack you with darkness. He did it to me. Tribulations and trials will come upon you. The Bible says in James

1:3, "The trying of your faith worketh patience." Troubles sometimes will come and the enemy will try to cut you because he doesn't want you to have a breakthrough, especially in the area of finances.

Perhaps a close friend will argue with you and say, "You're out of your mind." "You are just as crazy as you can be." "You are stupid." They may be broke, but they want to tell you to stop believing all that stuff.

Another thing you will find in this parable is offense. In Matthew 13:21 it says "By and by he is offended." When you become offended, the enemy has tied your hands. God loves a cheerful giver, but not an offended giver.

So as Ecclesiastes 11:6 says, "As thou knowest not what is the way of the [wind], nor how the bones grow in the womb of her that is with child; even so thou knowest not the works of God, who maketh all."

We are still talking about the seed principle here. The things the enemy uses against the Word as a seed, the things he used against Christ as a seed, are the same things he is going to use against your financial seed.

"The cares of this world." You cannot get caught up in the cares of this world if you are going to be a professional sower. The enemy will say, "That sofa is nice. Why not buy it instead of paying your tithe? They may not have that sofa later when you get the money." But listen to the Holy Ghost. The Lord will provide more sofas than you can use in your lifetime.

Another thing, "the deceitfulness of riches" will keep you from going on to your riches. Riches will deceive you. Riches will mislead you. First Timothy 6:16-19 says not to be high minded and trust in uncertain riches, because riches are deceitful. Money is deceitful without the proper anointing.

Never underestimate the power of a seed. If you do, you are underestimating God. You are underestimating Jesus, you are underestimating the Word of God and the Holy Ghost. You are underestimating them all. You are underestimating the cross, the death, the burial, and the resurrection of Jesus. Jesus went down as a seed and came up as a harvest.

They told Jesus He was finished. But it's just like when you plant your seed, you have to die to it. We do not want the seed, we want the harvest. The seed has to die for the harvest to come. And how does the seed die? By us turning it loose.

One of the biggest reasons we underestimate the power of the seed is that we do not understand the seed principle God has set for us to operate on His behalf in the earth realm. The church is supposed to be operating on the principle of God's Word until Jesus comes, because He *is* coming back.

Satan will make you believe he can keep you broke because he kept you broke for so long. He'll make you think that this is just another teaching. No, this is not just another teaching; this is breakthrough, like that seed broke through the concrete.

I think you will see this better if we remember again in Mark 4, when Jesus taught about the Word in this parable. Realize that He was also telling us about every facet of every way to use the seed. The enemy to the Word is the same enemy to the financial seed you sow. The enemy that would keep you from getting saved is the same enemy that works against the entire covenant. One of the things I've learned in my years of ministry is to recognize the enemy and know who is blocking you. You will need faith and understanding and, step by step, do what the Lord tells you to do.

The reason I used the slot machine illustration earlier is because, as Jesus said in Luke 16:8, the children of the world are wiser than the children of light. Those people keep putting money in the slot machine until they hit the jackpot.

So, when the wind is blowing and the cloud is showing up, keep on sowing. Sow in the morning, sow in the evening, because you never know when your seed is going to hit.

CHAPTER EIGHT

Understanding Due Season

There is always an appointed time, as seen in Ecclesiastes 3:1-8, especially with the law of seedtime and harvest. There is a time to sow and a time to reap, and there is a time in between. What you do with that time in between is very important.

1 To every thing there is a season, and a time to every purpose under the heaven:

2 A time to be born, and a time to die; a time to plant, and a time to pluck up that which is planted;

3 A time to kill, and a time to heal; a time to break down, and a time to build up;

4 A time to weep, and a time to laugh; a time to mourn, and a time to dance;

5 A time to cast away stones, and a time to gather stones together; a time to embrace, and a time to refrain from embracing;

6 A time to get, and a time to lose; a time to keep,
   and a time to cast away;
7 A time to rend, and a time to sew; a time to
   keep silence, and a time to speak;
8 A time to love, and a time to hate; a time of
   war, and a time of peace.

Look at how often the word "time" is used. You need to consider that and understand "the timing" of God, "the season" of God. If you don't understand that, you will become perturbed in every walk of life because your time is not the same as God's time. The key is that there is a "time" for everything. If you understand set-up, then you know the time will come.

The enemy has created so much frustration, so much giving up, and so much despondency because we do not understood "due season." We do not understood how the "kingdom of God" works. The Amplified Bible says, in Matthew 33, that the "kingdom of God" is God's way of doing things and this kingdom is within you. Therefore, God's ways of doing things are on the inside of you. And "God's way of doing things" is through faith, seedtime, and harvest.

Genesis 8:22 reveals more truth to us about sowing and reaping:

While the earth remaineth, seedtime and harvest, and cold and heat, and summer and winter, and day and night shall not cease.

This scripture makes it plain that while the earth remains, seedtime and harvest shall not cease. Once you get a revelation of "due season," you are all set.

Be not deceived; God is not mocked: for whatsoever a man soweth, that shall he also reap (Galatians 6:7).

"Be not deceived" is the deception of the devil. This verse promises, "Whatever a man soweth, that *shall* he also reap."

It is not *if* I reap, or *if* there will be a due season. It is *when!* This might not sound too heavy but it is saying something. The laws work, so there is going to be a due season. What will you be doing between "I believe" and "I receive?" There is a space in between and in that space is where you will have your greatest challenge. This is where the enemy will give you problems. You will say "I believe . . . I receive," and it looks like nothing is happening but there is always a "there it is." Therefore, you don't want "if" on your mind, wondering *if* it is going to come, but *when*. And it will be there in due time because the Lord knows when you are ready for it.

Here is another thing you should understand or you will be thrown by the enemy. "Due season" is not necessarily *your* season. You do not set the clock on this. Why? Because God is getting things in order. He has something else for you to get first and it all has to arrive at the same time. If we work with God properly, the enemy will be so confused that he'll just say, "I can't stop them." He may worry you and annoy you a little, but he can't stop you. He knows when you come into dominion, and he may try to throw a wrench in the works, but eventually he has to take it out. God has your due season divinely planned and it will be at the right time.

You need to come to the point that you have expectation every time you sow, and will not turn it loose because you have God's word on it that you will receive. Due season is not your season. God can hold back everything you thought was going to happen—those deadlines and all that stuff coming against you.

This statement will cause you to be a millionaire because God wants you to think a certain way. The key to operating God's law and to avoid frustration and the temptation to quit is to understand that with God there is an appointed time and due season for everything. (Ecc 3:1-8) There are spiritual laws that we operate with—the law of seedtime and harvest, the law of faith and the law of the covenant of increase. All these spiritual laws have to be understood and acted upon to receive benefits beyond this natural realm. If you have done what the Scriptures have told you to do, then wait (this isn't like waiting for a bus, but waiting on the Lord). This means while you wait, you are busy praising Him and doing what He wants you to do.

You must understand that this system does not operate in the natural way, such as weeks or months. God can do it without time. Go back to Galatians 6:7-10:

7 **Be not deceived; God is not mocked: for whatever a man soweth, that shall he also reap.**

8 **For he that soweth to his flesh shall of the flesh reap corruption; but he that soweth to the Spirit shall of the Spirit reap life everlasting.**

9 **And let us not be weary in well doing; for in due season we shall reap, if we faint not.**

10 **As we have, therefore, opportunity, let us do good unto all men, especially unto them especially unto them who are of the household of faith.**

Verse 9 says, "Let us not be weary in well doing: for in due season we shall reap, if we faint not." In other words, if we faint, we shall not reap. It is very easy to faint in this financial area as the enemy will put pressure on us when we are trying to come out of that hole. It's very easy to faint if what we want doesn't show up on Friday or when someone says we have to have it. But understand this: God controls that person making the demand and everything else, and if we line up with Him, what we need will come on time.

"Let us not be weary in well doing." The most well-doing thing would be obeying God and operating in obedience to your finances. Stop trying to figure out how you pay for this. Just listen to God and whatever He says to you, do it with whatever you have now. We call this trust, relying on God. It will get us off the world's system. You can't wait; you have to trust God now.

The Holy Ghost is saying to you, "Whatever you have now, whatever He says to you to do with it, do it, and you will jump systems." You need to understand the law of progression, you are taking something that is not completely grown yet. In other words, somebody gives you $5,000 and you run and tell everybody; however, you were believing for $50,000. All this means is that you have to plant more seed. God wants this money to circulate within the household of faith.

> **As we have, therefore, opportunity, let us do good unto all men, especially unto them who are of the household of faith (Galatians 6:10).**

What do we do now between "I believe" and "I receive?" We need to do something with that spot in between. What do you do? I'm getting a little faint, I have prayed, I have sung, but it still doesn't feel like I am making it. God does not faint or get weary. We see in Isaiah 40:28 that "the everlasting God, the LORD, the Creator of the ends of the earth, fainteth not, neither is weary? There is no searching of his understanding." We have the characteristics of God on the inside of us.

The first four words of Isaiah 40:28 ask, "Hast thou not known?" You have to know that God is *not* a man that He should lie (Numbers 23:19). If He said it, He will make it good, and He will hold everything back until it happens. What this verse is asking is, "Have you not known? Do you know God? Do you know what God can do for you?" You can almost say, as Solomon, that this is the conclusion of the whole matter. If you are going to get into the flow, there are some things you will have to know.

He giveth power to the faint; and to them that have no might he increaseth strength (Isaiah 40:29).

Here you have sown and you are waiting to reap, but things are creeping in upon you. However, He gives power to the faint, power to those who are about to quit. He puts more fuel in you so you won't quit. Isaiah goes on to say:

30 **Even the youths shall faint and be weary, and the young men shall utterly fall:**
31 **But they that wait upon the LORD shall renew their strength; they shall mount up with wings like eagles; they shall run, and not be weary; and they shall walk, and not faint (Isaiah 40:30-31).**

They *shall* and they *will* not faint. Everything I am telling you, I know it works if we operate God's laws properly because I have worked them myself. Take Ecclesiastes 3:1: "To everything there is a *season* and a time to every purpose under the heaven"; and connect that with Galatians 6:9: "And let us not be weary in well doing: for in *due season* we shall reap, if we faint not"; and Isaiah 1:19: "If ye be willing and obedient you shall eat the good of the land".

There are four things you must remember: 1) In due season; we shall reap if we faint not; 2) God has a due season; 3) His season is not our season; and 4) We shall reap.

What you have to understand, my brothers and sisters, is that whenever you switch systems, you need to make some adjustments. Anytime you switch jobs, you may have to move to another location, to a different setting. You have to make adjustments. You have to make an even bigger adjustment when you switch from your job being your *source* to your job being your *seed*. It will take some requirements on your spirit to be anointed with the ability of God to make the transition.

Here is what you do between "I believe—I receive" and "there it is." **With great expectation, "rejoice evermore"** (1 Thessalonians 5:16). The reason you rejoice is because you have inside information. Don't be looking at those bills all day long. Look at the Bible, look at what God has promised. Rejoice means brighten up, spin around, and leap. Revelation of any aspect of God is money in the bank. This is what you do between "I believe—I receive" and "there it is."

One of the worst things that can happen to you is to think you know but you don't know. If you think you know and you don't, then when the real thing comes along, you won't recognize it.

The passage below from Mark 4:26-29 is a powerful passage, especially when you look at the whole setting:

> **26 And he said, So is the kingdom of God, as if a man should cast seed into the ground;**
> **27 And should sleep, and rise night and day, and the seed should spring and grow up, he knoweth not how.**
> **28 For the earth bringeth forth fruit of herself; first the blade, then the ear, after that the full corn in the ear.**
> **29 But when the fruit is brought forth, immediately he putteth in the sickle, because the harvest is come.**

Someone has said, "A man's harvest in life depends entirely upon what he sows, and not upon what he has." Another way of saying this is, "A man's harvest in life depends entirely upon what he sows and what he *knows*." We need supernatural *knowledge* from God about money and supernatural *wisdom* from God about money. It is available to you because you are His child. But remember, you can't make a fool out of God because He knows everything.

In this kingdom you have to know what is the blade, what is the ear, and what is the full corn in the ear. Thus, God has to train us about money or we will be down the field trying to harvest an unmanifested crop. My daddy would go out in the field, pull one ear of corn open, and go back to the house because he knew it was not ready. But if he got a full corn in the ear, then he told the boys to bring the wagon down because the crop was ready to harvest. He didn't learn this overnight, however; he learned this from *his* daddy.

You, too, have to learn this process. Your life today is what it is because of what you have sown. And let me add here: There has been a lot of sowing without reaping. People have been giving, but they batter their giving by their mouth. As they sow their financial seed, they don't water it right. They began to talk about other people and God can't bring any seeds up with that because they have all those weeds in the field. What they need to do is to begin to say good things. This has to do with our spirit, soul, and body.

The devil operates by the same principle of sowing and reaping. He can't create anything, but he can pervert what has already been created. You may sow a good seed financially and look to God for the reaping, but then you say something satanic or negative, and the devil takes that principle and gives you his harvest and stops God's harvest. When you violate God's principle, that gives the devil permission (Satan *has* to get permission before he can touch you) to ruin your harvest. Then you have a space of repentance. If you don't operate and function in that space of repentance, the Lord's hand is tied and He allows you to experience some type of catastrophe.

Whatever you have in life came from a seed. Don't deceive yourself. The whole system works on seedtime and harvest. So whatever you have in life, you planted a seed for it. I see some people going down the field with a shovel right now, saying, "I am digging this thing up," because they don't want it to come up.

I'll never be broke another day in my life, and you don't have to be either. Your wallet can be empty, but you don't have to be broke. Once you get locked into this thing, you can't even think "broke." You keep holding on to tenacity and that boldness is going to start multiplying and the laws of increase are going to kick in. The Lord can't stand a person to walk in favor without doing something about it.

Again let me say, "I'll never be broke another day in my life!" The devil can't stop God. You are releasing your increase and your faith. You have decided, "I'm not going to be broke!" You say it first, and you will have it after. The enemy, not God, wants you to say you're broke.

Genesis 1:11 says,

And God said, Let the earth bring forth grass, the herb yielding seed, and the fruit tree yielding fruit after his kind, whose seed is in itself, upon the earth: and it was so.

"Fruit after its kind." You plant a money seed and money comes!" Every seed produces after its kind.

Don't look at other people with jealousy because you don't know what they had to do to get where they are. In other words, don't judge my harvest until you have seen my seed. Everything came from a seed that somebody planted, nothing just happens. *You have to plant!* The Lord can't send something unless you plant something. You are not going to get out of this world system automatically. This book can't change you unless you act upon what you read here. You have to plant a seed and water that seed. Then you have to know what to do between sowing and harvest time.

I want to remind you again that it is not *if* due season is coming, it is *when*, because due season with God always comes. We have to get a concept of this seed. The Word of God is a seed. Jesus was a seed. The Lord's whole system deals with a seed. First Peter 1:21 says, "Being born again, not of corruptible seed, but of incorruptible, by the word of God, which liveth and abideth forever."

The reason God keeps dealing with this topic (see Hebrews 11:3 and 1 Peter 1:21) is that "corruptible seeds" can be destroyed. Once you understand the laws of seedtime and harvest, and that your job is not your source—your job is the place where you get seed—then you can begin to walk a journey in total submission to God in the area of finances, placing whatever you have now in His hand and doing whatever He says to you to do with it. Your financial seed becomes incorruptible, indestructible, and your return cannot be annihilated. God puts a divine army around your manifestation and escorts it until it gets into your hands. Everything and everyone that tries to rob the armored car driver who is on his way to you has to deal with divine beings, because he has a divine destiny that has been assigned to him by the Father to bring it to your address.

Your seed becomes incorruptible and indestructible because you are in the divine will for God, and He becomes responsible for that seed to bring up a crop. He is also responsible to help you get it into the barn. There are angels right now trying to get some things to you, and the devil doesn't like it.

Satan cannot create words but he can pervert them. He wants to prevent God's Word from coming to pass. God has given us His Word and His words are creative. Planting seeds with the knowledge that you have received will cause prevailing harvest. "Prevailing harvest" means it can't be stopped.

In the beginning was the Word, and the Word was with God, and the Word was God (John 1:1).

The Word created everything and everything was created by the seed of the Word. Thus, everything is subject to the Word, including money.

The seed didn't come out of the harvest, the harvest came out of the seed. We are trying to draw from mercy, grace, goodness, kindness and the loving aspect of God, but we can't in this area of money. God can't give us anything without a seed. The Bible says God is a good

God, but it doesn't matter how much you praise Him and no matter how good you think you are living, you cannot tap into the harvest without a seed.

Yes, God has ways to get it to you. But until you tap in and do what He tells you to do, it will be a violation of spiritual law if God permits you to be wealthy without obedience.

You also have to learn how to wait. You can learn the part about giving, but you have to learn how to wait properly. While you are waiting, you may become discouraged and start saying a lot of foolish things, but God knows your timing and due season. He knows when to open the windows and He knows when you can take it. You might think you can take it tomorrow, but it might not be. All of my blessings are on schedule. If I had received them earlier, I probably would have acted like a fool and messed somebody up. But they are on schedule; therefore, I have no struggles with having them, I have no struggles with giving, and I have no struggles with what anyone says about me. I am enjoying them and I am going to keep them because God gave them to me and no one can take them away.

We understand everything else until it comes down to money. Then we get flaky and want money to stay in our pocket and come in our pocket. When you give God an offering, it is an offer. He doesn't have to accept your offering, especially when you didn't listen and give what He told you to give.

Now remember this—the seed didn't come out of the harvest, the harvest came out of the seed. Your harvest is in the seed. God has been trying to get it to you, but He couldn't because he has to have a seed, a proper attitude and a proper gratitude.

The Word was not in the begging, the Word was in the beginning. The church has to get rid of a beggarly spirit because it repels giving. People can pick up vibes when you are begging. Get rid of that beggarly spirit; it stinks. Get a farming spirit and plant.

Meditate on these three verses found in Mark 4:30-32:

30 And he said, To what shall we liken the kingdom of God? Or with what comparison shall we compare it?
31 It is like a grain of mustard seed, which, when it is sown in the earth, is less than all the seeds that are in the earth:
32 But, when it is sown, it groweth up, and becometh greater than all herbs, and shooteth out great branches, so that the fowls of the air may lodge under the shadow of it.

Read verse 32 again: "But when it is sown, it groweth up, and becometh greater." Get your mind off the mustard seed. It is there only to let you see a seed and how it operates.

Say! My due season is on the way. I am out of here. Out of debt! Out of distress! Out of discouragement! Out of discontentment!

We know now that it is not just by the mercies of God, not just by the grace of God, not just by your prayers and your meditation. There must be some *action* on your part in this area. If I had preached about healing, I would give you an opportunity to get healed. Now I am giving you an opportunity to plant and receive a bountiful financial harvest.

CHAPTER NINE

Keys to Receiving Your Due Season

To everything there is a season, and a time to every
purpose under the heaven: A time to be born, and a
time to die; a time to plant, and a time to pluck up that
which is planted; A time to kill, and a time to heal; a
time to break down, and a time to build up; A time to
weep, and a time to laugh; a time to mourn, and a time
to dance; A time to cast away stones, and a time to
gather stones together; a time to embrace, and a time
to refrain from embracing; A time to get, and a time to
lose; a time to keep, and a time to cast away; A time to
rend, and a time to sew; a time to keep silence, and a
time to speak; A time to love, and a time to hate; a time
of war, and a time of peace.
ECCLESIASTES 3:1-8

To everything there is a season, a time, and a purpose.
God has a purpose for His children being prosperous. It is
a purpose in finances. It is a divine purpose. Solomon also
says there is a "time." If you obtain something before your
season, it will do more harm than good.

Genesis 8:22 helps us understand due season.

While the earth remaineth, seedtime and harvest, and cold and heat, and summer and winter, and day and night shall not cease.

You are not going to understand this unless you understand how the kingdom of God operates. God's timing is not your timing; it is a timing He has set up. "Due season" is talking about manifestation and appointed time.

Habukkuk 2:3,4 says:

3 **For the vision is yet for an appointed time, but at the end it shall speak, and not lie: though it tarry, wait for it; because it will surely come, it will not tarry.**
4 **Behold, his soul that is lifted up is not upright in him: but the just shall live by his faith.**

Even though Habukkuk is talking here about a vision, it deals with an appointed time or due season. You can see the principle clearly.

Paul also wrote to the Galations in Galations 6:7,9:

7 **Be not deceived; God is not mocked: for whatsoever a man soweth, that shall he also reap.**

9 **And let us not be weary in well doing: for in due season we shall reap, if we faint not.**

"If you faint not," due season will come. Due season always come with God. It isn't *if,* but *when,* because it is definitely going to come.

In Habukkuk 2:3 where it says, "for the vision is yet for an appointed time," right here think about money, seeds you have planted. It may "tarry" a little while but "wait for it," because it will "surely come." We are dealing with God, not some bank which might go out of business. God doesn't go out of business. He is the only one who can use this word "surely." That should help you realize that it will not tarry, meaning it will not be too late. Even though the pressure might come on you, the Lord says it will be on time. You are not going under. What you do between "I believe" and "there it is" doesn't mean you sit around waiting, not doing anything. You keep working on your seed, you keep planting more seed and thank God for His goodness.

The key to operating God's law and avoiding frustration and the temptation to quit is to understand that with God there is an appointed time and a due season for everything. That is why Ecclesiastes says that there is a time for this and a time for that. We must understand this timing. The temptation to quit will come, but "faint not" means "don't quit." The enemy will try to send a lot of bluff your way, but you are loaded. You have planted your seed, made the declaration *"Money Cometh!"*, and claimed the amount that you need. You have told Satan to take his hands off your money, and told ministering spirits to cause the money to come in.

The Lord told me that those prophetic words *"Money Cometh"* means a continual process of money is coming in, and it also means making a demand on money, because money has to obey us. God does not want us to go without finances. You have to get this thing in your heart to understand it and if you need money, you have to plant a seed. So use those words *"Money Cometh,"* because that promise is given to the Body of Christ. Find a seed, find some good soil, plant where the Lord tells you, and He will help you. Then claim what you want from Him and tell Satan to take his hands off your money.

Understanding Mark 4:26-29 is so vital. You must meditate on these scriptures.

> **26 And he said, So is the kingdom of God, as if a man should cast seed into the ground;**
> **27 And should sleep, and rise night and day, and the seed should spring and grow up, he knoweth not how.**

28 For the earth bringeth forth fruit of itself; first the blade, then the ear, after that the full corn in the ear.

29 But when the fruit is brought forth, immediately he putteth in the sickle, because the harvest is come.

Under the mercy and grace of God you can survive without sowing, but only in the gleaning part of the field, the part that is left after the harvest for the vagabonds, those who don't know how to sow.

As you read Mark 4, starting with verse 26, you'll see the words "as if a man," making a comparison. I will put a little more emphasis on verse 27, because the man went about his business, "should sleep, and rise night and day." He didn't just sit around. He continued with his regular routine with the work that he had to do, and he took care of the seed also. "And the seed should spring and grow up, he knoweth not how." When you get into "due season" and get into real money, you may not know how you did it, but you have to stop trying to figure out who will give it to you. Don't be concerned about that, just go and do what you have to do. If you don't try to figure this out, that means your job becomes your source.

When he says "he knoweth not how," it means he doesn't know how that seed came up. But the seed is made to come up. Then he says "for the earth bringeth forth fruit of itself." The system is set up to work. Just like the earth is set up to work with a seed to produce a harvest, God has his system set up with a financial seed to bring a harvest.

One thing we must be careful not to do is try to harvest too fast, ahead of due season. The Lord blesses you with $5,000, but you are believing for $50,000. If this happens, just ask the Lord, "What do you want me to do with this?" and He'll show you more ground in which to plant more seed. Then you'll have more than one thing working for you. It is very easy to have plenty of money using this system.

Mark 4:28 says, "For the earth bringeth forth fruit of itself; first the blade, then the ear, after that the full corn in the ear." This verse gives us three seasons; we just have to know when to put the sickle in.

5 Keys to Receiving Your Due Season

5 **Trust in the LORD with all thine heart; and lean not unto thine own understanding.**
6 **In all thy ways acknowledge him, and he shall direct thy paths.**

7 Be not wise in thine own eyes: fear the LORD, and depart from evil.
8 It shall be health to thy navel, and marrow to thy bones.
9 Honor the LORD with thy substance, and with the first fruits of all thine increase:
10 So shall thy barns be filled with plenty, and thy presses shall burst out with new wine (Proverbs 3:5-10).

Key #1 – *Honoring the Lord*

In order to honor the Lord you have to obey the Lord. The command in Proverbs 3:9 says to "honor the LORD with thy substance" and then the writer specifies how he wants you to do it—"with the first fruits of *all* thine increase." The Lord tells you what to do, there is an activating power, you have to do it. As you give your tithes, write it down so you can know how much to expect. In your time of praying and confessing, take out the book and say, "Lord, here it is. This is what I have given, and expect." When you tithe, you still should press. Don't become satisfied because you are a tither. You cannot give what you want to give; you give what the Lord tells you to give, "of all thine increase." The Lord never tells you to do something without His doing something in return. We must activate verse 9 in our lives before we confess verse 10:

So shall thy barns be filled with plenty, and thy presses shall burst out with new wine. (Proverbs 3:10)

Whether you see something or not, just do it and you will qualify. If you heed these two verses, your barns will be filled with plenty and your presses with new wine. That means breaking out of the wall of containment. But, as shown in Mark 4, it is a law of progression, a process. It will not happen overnight.

Key #2 – *Speak to your seed*

You have to guard your confession all the time. Consider your ways, for it is a violation of all spiritual laws for you to sow much and bring in little.

Lets look at Haggai 1:5,6

5   Now, therefore, thus saith the LORD of hosts; *Consider your ways.*

6   Ye have sown much, and bring in little; ye eat, but ye have not enough; ye drink, but ye are not filled with drink; ye clothe yourself, but there is none warm; and he that earneth wages earneth wages to put it into a bag with holes.

Whose house is first, your house or God? Are you sending tithes and special offerings to His house? Do men and women of God have a good place to preach and call in souls to the kingdom? Are you paying your house note and not paying your tithe? You say, "God gave it to me." But there is a difference between the 10 percent and tithing. The 10 percent is the tithe, but tithing is different than the tithe. You give 10 percent—that's the tithe, but then you have to say something, speak over your tithe, speak to your seed. Don't just pluck your money in the bucket. Let's look at Haggai 1:2-5:

2   Thus speaketh the Lord of hosts, saying: This people say, The time is not come, the time that the Lord's house should be built.
3   Then came the word of the Lord by Haggai the prophet, saying,
4   Is it time for you, O ye, to dwell in your cieled houses, and this house to lie in waste?
5   Now therefore thus sayth the Lord of hosts; Consider your ways.

The Lord is concerned about your house, He wants things in perspective. He wants you to get your priorities straight. Now read Haggai 1:6-7:

6 Ye have sown much, and bring in little; ye eat, but ye have not enough; ye drink, but ye are not filled with drink; ye clothe yourself, but there is none warm; and he that earneth wages earneth wages to put it into a bag with holes.
7 Thus saith the LORD of hosts; Consider your ways.

Something is not right, because this violates all spiritual laws. "Ye have sown much, and bring in little." What you need to do is to consider your words.

Proverbs 24:27 tells us that when we get God's work established, then we can build our house. There is nothing wrong with having good things.

The Amplified Bible says it this way: "[Put first things first.] Prepare your work outside and get it ready for yourself in the field; and afterwards build your house and establish a home.

It is a violation to sow much and bring in little. Speak to your seed, know what to say, consider your ways, and continually speak.

Let them shout for joy, and be glad, who favor my righteous cause. Yea, let them say continually, Let the LORD be magnified, who hath pleasure in the prosperity of his servant (Psalms 35:27).

This is how you favor His righteous cause, by honoring the Lord with the first fruit of your increase. Or you can say, those "that favor my righteous cause . . . let them shout for joy, and be glad . . . Continually." Carolyn and I talked this stuff continually. We would say, "We don't have a need. All of our bills are paid, we have plenty of money, and we are able to give big." We kept talking it. When the Lord told me it was time to quit my job, my family members thought I had lost my mind. But I didn't ask for anything and they didn't give me anything. They started watching us and started coming over themselves.

What does it mean, "let the Lord be magnified"? Well, the Lord Himself doesn't need any magnification, so what is this verse talking about? You are bought with a price; therefore, glorify God in your body and in your spirit and in your lifestyle. Let the Lord be magnified, who has pleasure in the prosperity of His servants. When you are broke, the Lord is displeased because you are saying that He cannot take care of His own. *I'll never be broke another day in my life! Money Cometh to me now!*

Key #3 - *Speak to the mountain called debt*

What you have to know is that *debt* is a mountain.

> **For verily I say unto you, That whosoever shall *say* unto this mountain . . . (Mark 11:23).**

You have everything in motion. You can talk to the mountains all you want, but nothing will happen if you don't follow all the other things I told you. I have told you about the law of seedtime and harvest and due season, but here are some breakthrough keys to substantiate what you have done already. You have planted your seeds and obeyed God, and now you are between "I believe" and "there it is." Now you are talking to debt. Take your bills, add them up from the least to the greatest, and start paying the smallest one first. When you get that first small one paid off, write on there "paid in full," and dance a little bit. Then tell the next one, "You're next." There is something about paying off that first one. It brings a thrill because it lets you know you can do it.

Say you pay a $300 bill off, then the next one is $700, a piece of cake. Excitement is building up in you now and you go on down the line. When you get to that $7,000 bill, $7,000 doesn't mean any more than the $700 dollar one, or $700,000 is no different than $7,000. Now you are in a system and you understand the bigness of God, so money is just money now.

As Mark 11:23 says, speak to the mountain called debt. We have been talking to every mountain but the debt mountain. Say to it, "You have to go." The church uses Scripture about everything but money. We think we are violating spirituality to talk about money. Money has tricked us; it has been lying in the corner laughing at us because it knows we have authority over it. The devil also knows because it belongs to our Father. The Father has given us faith, the law of seedtime and harvest and tithing. Why do you think He put all of this in the system. So He can bypass the system and get you on His system.

Also keep talking, don't stop talking. Jesus talked to the root of the tree, you will have to talk to the root of your debt—the devil and his cohorts. For awhile they are going to flap their wings like they are not going to leave. But in the time that Jesus talked to the tree and left it, to the time He got back, the tree had dried up from the root. You know why? Jesus never turned it loose. It was a done deal. Some of you look and say, "Jesus didn't do any good. Some of those leaves are still green." It's the same way they watched Mt. Zion, that little church I was pastoring. They passed by in their cars and laughed and made fun, but I just kept on plowing. Even though I didn't know then what I know now, I knew I was headed somewhere and I kept on working. I would talk to that tree. It didn't look like it was dying, but it was dying all the time. God was just getting me to another level.

Key #4 – *Be aggressive*

Don't stop talking to the mountain until it leaves. In Mark 10:46-52, blind Bartimaeus cried out to God even though those around him told him to stop it. But he was aggressive; he kept on doing it. He kept saying, "Jesus, thou Son of David . . . Many charged him that he should hold his peace" but he didn't listen. He just kept crying out to Jesus.

We see also in Mark 5:25-34 that the woman with the issue of blood never stopped talking. She was aggressive and she got what she came for.

Another example is given in Luke 5:17-20 where the men brought in a bed on which was a man who was sick with a palsy, these men cut a hole in the roof to let him down. That was aggressive, my brothers and sisters.

Do whatever it takes, whatever the spirit of God leads you to do. One time I committed a wrong against a man and wanted to make it right. God told me to give him $100. So I went to his house (which was bigger than mine; I didn't have what I have now), but they told me he was at the steakhouse. Now understand, I needed this $100 myself, but I had to obey. So I went to the steakhouse, and he was eating a porterhouse steak so big it was hanging off the plate. It was test time. "Will you do what I tell you to do?" I went up to him (he was with another businessman), and I said, "The Lord told me to give you this" and I just slipped the money into his hand. I knew that I had obeyed God and I knew there was coming a time when I was going to be sitting at the same place eating a steak, because someone who had committed a wrong against me was going to make it right in the same way. This has happened to me over and over and over again. I have been sitting in a place and somebody has walked up to me and said, "No! You can't pay this, I got it," because I had obeyed God. There are some tests you will fail. You want to argue with God, but when He tells you to do something, your heart has to be in it—not your head—because the Lord is going to test you. He will test you to see if He can trust you first with what you have now. It is the giving, but more the obedience of where you are.

Key #5 – *Consistency is the key to breakthrough*

Whatever you do, keep doing it, don't stop. Consistency is the key to breakthrough.

CHAPTER TEN

Your Source of Power: Your Job or God?

*"For I know the plans I have for you," declares the
LORD, "plans to prosper you, and not to harm you,
plans to give you hope and a future"*
JEREMIAH 29:11 (NIV)

You need to understand and have it clear in your mind
that God does have a plan for you in the area of finances.
The first thing you must do is *focus.* According to Jeremiah
29:11, God's plan is to prosper you and to give you hope
and a future. If this is true—and it is—then why are so
many Christians in debt today? Let's study King David in
1 Samuel 22:1,2:

> 1 David, therefore, departed thence, and escaped
> to the cave Adullam: and when his brethren
> and all his father's house heard it, they went
> down thither to him.

2   And every one who was in distress, and every
    one who was in debt, and every one who was
    discontented, gathered themselves unto him;
    and he became a captain over them: and there
    were with him about four hundred men.

This lets you see the shape of Christians today. In these two verses David's family bore the mark of Christians in distress, in debt, discontentment—all of this because of money. A lot of this is due to our job system and the world system versus the Word system and God's system of finances. We need to escape from this mess. What we need to do is find out how to shift from one system to the other.

A better picture of how Christians should be is shown in Isaiah 61:9 (Amplified):

And their offspring shall be known among the nations, and their descendents among the peoples; all who see them [in their prosperity] will recognize and acknowledge that they are the people whom the Lord has blessed.

This verse shows where we are *supposed* to be but we are still in 1 Samuel 22:1,2. We have to get from 1 Samuel 22 to Isaiah 61:9 through Jeremiah 29:11. God already said He has plans, but somewhere these plans have been interrupted. A transition has to be made to get to Isaiah. Here are some prophetical words that the Lord gave me that will help you to understand:

"You must understand the difference between the two systems, and be willing to change. Recognize that the old system is not getting the job done, and spiritually separate yourself from the old system of finance and get in the new way of living."

If you continue to live in the world system of finance, with your job as your source, you will live all your life and never fulfill the plan God has for you. Never enjoy the place he has provided for you.

The only way God can bless you is through the Word. That means you must discover what the Word says, work that Word, and act on the Word. God works through His Word, so the only way He can bless you is that first, you get the Word, and second, you adhere to the Word. In the beginning was the Word, not all of this begging stuff.

In order for prosperity to work and for people to change their lives, our beginning will also have to be with the Word. But we begin with "religion." We got saved and we joined a religion, but that religion didn't tell us about the Word. I have good news for you: You can begin now with the Word.

Many have become very relaxed and do not understand the importance of tithing. Tithing is the covenant. If you don't tithe, you have no part with the covenant. Tithing is the covenant connector. *Not tithing* will stop the benefits of the covenant from flowing your way and you will be on your own. This is where many are today and it has been rough for them when it comes to money. We have been on our own, sometimes with two or three jobs or a business, and none of it is producing.

Malachi 3:10 says,

Bring all the tithes into the storehouse, that there may be meat in mine house, and prove me now herewith, saith the LORD of hosts, if I will not open for you the windows of heaven, and pour out for you a blessing, that there shall not be room enough to receive it.

The verse preceding this warns, "Ye are cursed with a curse, for ye have robbed me . . ." (verse 9).

In the original language, verse 9 means, "You are cursed with a curse; this is our final notice that your contract has been terminated."

Many people have their job as their source, trying to make a living, but all you are doing is making a killing. You are killing yourself trying to make your job supply your needs but it will not. Where is your loyalty?

People have jobs and they are committed to those jobs. They do things on the job that they wouldn't do for God. They set their clocks, so they can be on time. They make sure they are dressed properly for that job. They are diligent. You can make $50,000 or $80,000 a year, but as long as you make the job your source, the check is still not going to be enough. Why? If you get a better job, if you are not in the system of God, you will outspend it. You say, "I'll get this job and stay on the same level," but you don't. You may do it for a few months, but then you began to think about the extra cash you'll receive by going to a higher level, and you spend it before you make it. So even though you are bringing in more money, it is never going to be enough.

The farmer gets the seed and brings it home, but he doesn't pay his light bill or his house note with it. What does he do with the seed? He plants it and lives off the harvest. You have been trying to live off the seed. That is why you are having such a struggle. Your paycheck is only your seed. Take the seed and do like the farmer. You are trying to meet all your needs with a paycheck that is not meant to meet your needs. *God* wants to meet your needs.

The children of Israel came out of Egypt as millionaires but they had nowhere to spend the money. God said to them, "I'm the man, I'll take care of you. I'll put you in a place where you will not be able to spend it, so I can show you who is your source." We know that their shoes didn't wear out or their clothes, manna fell from the sky, and there was no one sick. God just showered blessings upon them. So by the time they got to where they could spend the money, God showed them who He was.

The world has caused us to buy into this thinking that our paycheck will take care of us. We see the job as our supply, but the check wasn't meant to be our supply. God was meant to be our supply. The check is only supposed to buy the seed. Take the seed you planted and live off of the harvest. This is God's way.

When you ultimately make God your source instead of your job, you will be more interested in doing it God's way than in doing it the world's way. When you shift, you know you have shifted because godly things are now more important to you.

In order for you to get into God's way of operating, you will have to do what God told Abraham in Genesis 12:1:

Now the LORD had said unto Abram, Get thee out of thy country, and from thy kindred, and from thy father's house, unto a land that I will show thee.

What the Lord is trying to show here is "a land," a new way of living. He wants you to see that the family unit was the source of prosperity at that time. Wealth was there, but the Lord said, "Come out and do it My way because that wealth is not going to be used My way."

He was saying to Abraham, "Get out from the world's system of operating where this wealth is concerned. Come out of the world's way of doing things."

Until you are willing to divorce your old system of operation, you will never be ready to go full steam ahead in God's system of operations; you will always see your job and your paycheck as your source that takes care of you instead of God being your source. We need to trust God and do it His way. Remember, God said in Jeremiah that He has a plan, but He can't fulfill His plan if you don't get into His system.

God makes it very plain how He will deal with your needs. If your paycheck is your source, then you are limited on what you can get with that paycheck. When you run out of what that paycheck says—and you'll do it fast—you can go no farther.

God wants you to break free from the world's limited system. Thank You, Jesus! He wants to break you free from the walls that are containing you because "*You're not broke; you have a seed!*"

CHAPTER ELEVEN

Sowing for a Living?

We know that the Word is a seed, but we are talking about financial prosperity. One aspect of prosperity is that God has a covenant of increase for his children. We see in Genesis 8:22, "While the earth remaineth, seedtime and harvest, and cold and heat, and summer and winter and day and night shall not cease," and the earth has not ceased. It is still here.

We also understand that the Lord's way of doing things is seedtime and harvest. Your job is not your source, but for many of us, that is all we know. We are trying to make the job our source or get it some other way, but God wants us to go His way. That is the only way He can back us up. Let's take another look at Mark 4:26-28:

> **26 And he said, So is the kingdom of God, as if a man should cast seed into the ground;**

27 And should sleep, and rise night and day, and
the seed should spring and grow up, he
knoweth not how.

28 For the earth bringeth forth fruit of itself; first
the blade, then the ear, after that the full corn
in the ear.

In Mark's Gospel, "the kingdom of God" is God's way
of doing things, but it is a mystery. You have to understand
the mystery "as if a man should cast seed into the ground
. . . he knoweth not how." This "kingdom of God" is the
same "kingdom of God" that we are to seek in Matthew
6:33. Now he is going to tell you how to get into that
kingdom in the aspect of finances. "As if a man should
cast seed into the ground," then that man goes on about
his Father's business. Then he should "sleep and rise night
and day and the seed should spring and grow up and he
knoweth not how"—"first the blade, then the ear, after
that the full corn in the ear."

> But when the fruit is brought forth, immediately
> he putteth in the sickle, because the harvest is
> come (Mark 4:29).

Basically, what we are saying here is that you won't get
a harvest if you don't know how to plant.

Now he that ministereth seed to the sower both minister bread for your food, and multiply your seed sown, and increase the fruits of your righteousness (2 Corinthians 9:10).

But my God shall supply all your need according to his riches in glory by Christ Jesus (Philippians 4:19).

It is so important that we understand these two basic scriptures—2 Corinthians 9:10 and Philippians 4:19. And in order for these two scriptures to work in your life, you have to sow. You have to become a sower in order to become a reaper. People have tried to reap where they have not sown. The first thing you have to do is either sow or give.

"My God shall supply all your need," but not if you don't give him a seed. Your needs do not move God. If they did, He would go and feed hungry people all over the world. But someone has to first go to other countries with a seed. Read again, "He ministereth seed to the sower," and also go back to Genesis 8:22, the law of seedtime and harvest. It *is* a law.

Psalm 23:1 says, "The LORD is my shepherd; I shall not want," but again, not if we don't give any seed. That is why we have been in so much want. We take the verse because it sounds good, but we are lazy and we want something for nothing. We are in the church with a welfare mentality, and the Lord doesn't like welfare. He tells you to get a job and get some seeds so you can plant it.

We are living a mediocre life with one house, two cars, and many bills. We are coming out of that situation. Get this revelation of seedtime and harvest. The eyes of your understanding need to be enlightened in this area. We have been messing around with this money thing for centuries and we have not taken our wealth yet. But there is a breed rising up that will make that wealth move.

The Bible says in Psalms 112 that a man who walks upright shall have wealth and riches in his house. A lot of people love God and are not practicing sin, but they are broke. What is supposed to be in your house? Wealth and riches are supposed to be in your house. In Proverbs 13, we see that the wealth of the wicked is laid up for the just. How long have we been saying that? It needs to move. Who will move it, informed going-and-doing-it Christians? You have to move it according to the law of seedtime and harvest.

Here are three things you must understand about sowing for a living: 1) A sower is not just somebody who plants every now and then; 2) A sower sows for a living just as a farmer farms for a living; and 3) When you commit yourself to become a sower, God commits Himself to become a supplier.

A genuine sower has every dollar on the block every time. He is ready to sow at all times. Always available with all he has to let God have it. Always asking, "What do you want me to do, Lord?" God is looking for sowers to sow into, and he gets other sowers to sow into *that* sower so that sower can sow into another sower, and on and on. When that gets to rolling, harvest comes next.

In order to qualify for God to be your supplier, you must become a bona fide sower. We are to be cheerfully looking, listening, watching, and willing.

Consider the seed, the ground and the farmer in Mark 4:3,4:

3   Behold, there went out a sower to sow.
4   And it came to pass, as he sowed, some fell by the wayside.

A lot of people feel that God is supposed to be meeting their needs and wonder why they are getting nothing back. Did you sow in a wayside deal? Just because you sow or give does not necessarily mean you will get something back.

You see that in this parable. The principles are there. Some didn't get anything because "the fowls of the air came and devoured it." The wayside ground.

The reason the fowls came and devoured this seed is because it wasn't planted deep enough in the ground. It wasn't covered up, it was too exposed. As a result, it was devoured. In the wayside ground, do you see harvest? No! You don't get harvest when you sow in wayside ground. When you sow your finances in shallow word ministries, you will not get any return because they are not the people God is sowing in.

The need should not move you to give. If you should be moved by a need, then God would be moving all the time. God is not moved by a *need*; God is moved by a *seed*. When you sow on wayside ground and shallow ground, your deposit will be stolen.

In the next type of soil, the seed couldn't develop roots because it was sown on stony ground. Thus, there was no harvest.

> 5 **And some fell on stony ground, where it had not much earth; and immediately it sprang up, because it had no depth of earth.**
> 6 **But when the sun was up, it was scorched; and because it had no root, it withered away (Mark 4:5-6).**

In the third type of soil, the seed was planted in a ground that had some depth to it. It wasn't wayside or stony ground, but it fell among thorns. You sow your seed where you know the word is going forth. Do not sow your seed to a begging television preacher.

> 7 **And some fell among thorns, and the thorns grew up, and choked it, and it yielded no fruit.**
> 8 **And other fell on good ground, and did yield fruit that sprang up and increased; and brought forth, some thirtyfold, and some sixty, and some an hundred (Mark 4:7-8).**

If you give when God tells you to give, it will propel you into wealth. You must give when and where God tells you to give. There is no increase in repay. When you give to the poor, He promised that He would repay you (Proverbs 19:17). Repay just gives back what you gave to the poor. God picks the soil, you do the sowing.

Based on Proverbs 3:9, "honoring the Lord," you go to God and ask, "What do you want me to give? Speak, God, and I'll obey." "If ye be willing and obedient, ye shall eat the good of the land" (Isaiah 1:19).

> **If they *obey and serve* him, they shall spend their days in prosperity, *and* their years in pleasures (Job 36:11).**

These are the guidelines for being a sower—obey and serve Him. Be a servant to Him with your money, do what He tells you to do. Job said, "They will spend their days in prosperity." Why? Because God is their supplier. Psalms 118:25 says, "Save now, I beseech thee, O LORD, I beseech thee, send now prosperity." God is sending prosperity now!

As a result of my going through that process, God has to honor me with plenty because now I am part of helping fulfill His covenant. This goes back to Proverbs, honoring the Lord with our first fruits, until all the families of the earth have been blessed.

We have to be careful about the ground we are sowing in or our seed will be in a ground where it will not produce a harvest. Good ground will cause increase. Only believers will believe this, a fool will not. The believers are to act upon the Word, line upon line.

One of our problems is that we are not listening; thus, these things have not taken root as they should. Let's take a look at Mark 4:9-13:

9 And he said unto them, He that hath ears to hear, let him hear.

10 And when he was alone, they that were about him with the twelve asked of him the parable.

11 And he said unto them, Unto you it is given to know the mystery of the kingdom of God: but unto them that are [outside], all these things are done in parables:

12 That seeing they may see, and not perceive; and hearing they may hear, and not understand; lest at any time they should be converted, and their sins should be forgiven them.

13 And he said unto them, Know ye not this parable? And how, then, will ye know all parables?

When Jesus said, "Know ye not this parable," He was telling them, "There is something within this teaching that lines up everything else and it explains the mystery of the kingdom." The way God gets us off of this system is that we do as He says. Let Him pick out the soil as He brought soil to Elijah. You have to put yourself in the position for God to be your supplier. And, as He promised in Philippians 4:19, He will supply *all* your needs.

Remember, *you're not broke; you have a seed.* Plant it today!

To order additional copies of

You're Not Broke You Have a Seed

send a check or money order in the amount of $12.99 plus $4.00 shipping and handling to:

Ever Increasing Word Ministries
P.O. Box 7
Darrow, LA 70725

or

call toll-free

888.238.WORD (9673)

or visit our website at

www.eiwm.org